King HEZEKIAH

Examining a Life of Bold Faith

Five-week Bible study guide
By: Jaclyn Rowe

jaclyn rowe

Life in Progress

Life in Progress Ministries
Potosi, MO 63664

Copyright © 2013 by Jaclyn Kelley Rowe
Published by Jaclyn Rowe, Life in Progress Ministries
Potosi, Missouri 63664

Library of Congress Control Number: 2013913984

ISBN 978-1-4675-8304-6

Printed in the United States of America.

Acknowledgements

To my Savior

I must give the utmost thanks to my Lord and Savior, Jesus Christ. Words cannot express the praise He merits. I could fill these pages and it would not be enough. Without Him, I can do nothing. I am so thankful Jesus rescued my soul, allowing the exchange of my sin for His righteousness and then giving me His Spirit as proof. Everything I hope for my life can be summed up in anticipation of *that day* when I see Him face to face. May He say, "Well, done!" for His is the only approval I seek.

To my Husband

You are my best friend. On this earth, you are the one to whom I cling for support, encouragement and sanity! I respect you and admire your love for our Lord and your desire to please Him. It is incredible to watch you with our children and easy to love you as my spouse. I could not and would not have finished this without you. Thank you for your continuous prayers, patience and partnership in ministry. I pray God will be glorified for years to come through our marriage, our ministry, our family and our home.

To some Special Women

Mom, thank you for everything. Without your willingness to babysit, read, edit, re-read and encourage, I would never get anything done. You have the heart of a servant and the gifting of an awesome teacher. So much of what I do as a speaker and teacher is by your example. You have always been a tremendous mother, my biggest fan and my forever friend. God has and will use you beyond what you see, not only in my life, but also in the lives of countless others. Your reach is remarkable.

Nicole, who knew when we first met as "enemies" on the basketball court that we would become the closest of friends? (Yes, I know, you way out-played me.) Thank you for reading this study and for encouraging me to listen to God's voice. Thank you for holding me accountable to all God requires and for praying. You are a woman of incredible strength. God's hand is so evident on your life. I look forward to many more years of friendship!

Mrs. Bev, what shall I say? Sitting under your teaching and learning God's word from you is a thrill in and of itself. But, even that does not compare to the impact you've had on this study. Thank you for your time. I recognize how precious a gift you have given. Thank you for your example of obedience and faithfulness to our great God.

To my little bro

It's so nice to have a built-in editor extraordinaire. Thanks for answering all my irritating questions and for the countless hours of theological discussion and mind-saving distraction. Together, I think we are easily too much for most people. I'm thankful for a brother like you and cannot wait to see how God rolls out His plans for your life and the ministry He has given us. You, as well as I, are a life in progress. Learn it. Love it. Live it!

Special Thanks to **Jerry Richards**, **Erica Peddi** and **Amy Locurto** for taking time to help me. This study is better because of you. I'm so grateful for your brilliant and creative minds! And to the many others who have encouraged and prayed for me along the way, thank you.

Table of Contents

Foreword

Although a young author, Jaclyn Rowe has grasped the gravity of our nation's situation — a nation that has lost its moorings. In this wonderful study, Jaclyn opens the account of Hezekiah in a way that encourages readers to see that the children of God, even in such a time as this, are not without hope.

She leads us on a journey that begins with the opening of the eyes of a king as he assesses with dismay the threat to Judah's future. The process is one we are encouraged to emulate personally and corporately as we hear Hezekiah crying out to God for deliverance from apostasy. We rejoice at the heart change of a people who respond to their godly king. Finally, hallelujah, we witness once again God's amazing willingness to restore a nation whose people will humble themselves, and pray and seek His face. Step by step, prayer by prayer, a nation is changed.

Open this study guide, follow Jaclyn's divinely inspired insight and begin your own journey of hope.

Bev McColloch

Women's Bible Study Leader

Introduction

When I was a little girl, my late Grandpa Ted would call me on a very specific day every year. Rather early in the morning my mother would enter my bedroom, phone in hand, and say, "Jaclyn, Grandpa Ted wants to talk to you." Reluctantly and half asleep, I would roll over and reach for the phone. "Hello?" is all I could speak with a weak and tired voice. On the other end, I would hear, "WAKE UP!" Grandpa would shout, "Have you looked outside today? It's snowing!" As a child, it wouldn't take me long to shake my drowsiness and leap to the window. I would throw back the curtains and gaze upon the fields only to find them just as they were the day before — without snow.

"April Fools!" That is what grandpa would laugh and snort and say. He was so proud of himself, year after year. If April Fools is meant to make you feel foolish, it worked. I'm thankful for the fun memories, but still surprised at how many years it took for me to catch on. I fell for it.

So many people are being fooled. Access to ideas, opinions, and information is at an all time high. It is more than we can fathom, and perhaps, more than we can handle. How do we know what is real and what is fake? How do we know what is fact and what is fiction? How do we know what is right and what is wrong? Conceivably, there are no greater questions our generation faces. In all the confusion and chaos we must conclude: we cannot *all* be right. Someone is right and someone is the fool.

TRUTH is what I want. What about you? I love the account of King Hezekiah. Through the study of His word, God has shown me amazing truths about Himself, His heart and His desires for His people. My hope and prayer is when you have completed this book, you will not only have learned new things, but will have experienced the hope of God at work in your own life, discovering in the end — TRUTH is a person.

About the Study

First, *King Hezekiah* may be done individually or with a group. It is designed to take five weeks — six if you want to use a week for introduction or a week for celebration. Please visit the *Small Groups* page on my website, www.jaclynrowe.com, for the **Leaders Guide** download and free tips, resources and information on how to form a Bible study group.

Each week, there are five lessons to study. If you are participating in a group, do each day's study on your own and then discuss what you learn when you meet. Each lesson varies from 10 to 35 minutes. The days are meant to build on one another, so please do not skip around. Look up the scriptures in your personal Bible. While our primary focus is in 2 Chronicles, Isaiah and 2 Kings, where the accounts of King Hezekiah are given, additional passages are layered in for deeper study and understanding. The first week is a set-up. You will not actually begin to study the history, context and life of Hezekiah until weeks two and three. This is intentional. Main ideas are centered on each page and **bold** lines require attention and action from the reader. Each day ends with an Application section. Application is your opportunity to personally apply each day's lesson and should be given serious consideration.

I would love to hear from you as you study. Feel free to find me at Life in Progress Ministries on Facebook via www.facebook.com/lipministries or via my website, www.jaclynrowe.com.

I'm praying for you.

Blessings!

Learn it. Love it. Live it.
Share it with your friends!

WEEK 1 – Establishing a Mindset

Day One

A Weak Mind

My dad is funny. On every family trip we have ever been on, without fail, my mother gets carsick. Like a broken record, my dad eagerly declares the reason for her misery, "you don't have a weak stomach; you have a weak mind." He never gets carsick.

I would like to begin our study by discussing this very topic — not preventing nausea in the car — but avoiding a weak mind.

It is my aspiration that anyone reading this Bible study be encouraged, taught and inspired by the Word of God. I will be the first to admit that in years past the majority of my personal study was centered on New Testament scriptures. Unintentionally, I had fallen into believing the New Testament scriptures were more relevant and easier to understand; so, I often avoided delving into Old Testament passages. The Old Testament scriptures *are* difficult to navigate. However, I have been amazed by how personally enlightening and meaningful the Old Testament accounts have been. I cannot wait for you to open the pages of your Bible and begin what has been a four-year journey for me.

I assume most people reading this would agree the Bible is God's word and is central to our Christian faith. My concern is we approach God's word too casually. If we are honest, we are not really expecting it to have significant impact on our thoughts, behaviors, relationships, ambitions, heart, body and soul. In fact, we are sometimes shocked by what we find.

Before we dive in, I feel it is crucial that you and I have a deep hunger and widened perspective concerning the entire Word of God. I have often made the mistake of entering a time of Bible study with a weak mindset. Out of obligation or a guilty conscience, I've cracked open the pages of God's word, read a few verses and checked the "done" box. Is it any wonder it takes me so long to see His word at work in my life?

Lose the Weak Mindset

We need a strong, intentional mindset to gain the most from this, or any other, study. No room for casualness here. I will tell you now it's going to be next week before we start studying the context and substance of the account of King Hezekiah. For this week, I feel God would like us to focus on a few key scriptures to get us on track and to ultimately answer an important question:

Why study a dated and forgotten character such as King Hezekiah?

Before we answer that question, please take a step away from our person of interest and do a quick exercise.

Define, in your own words, each of the following terms:

Instruction:

Endurance:

Encouragement:

Hope:

Based on your own definitions, which of the four do you need *most* at this season of your life? Why?

Now, open your Bible and read Romans 15:4, then answer the following questions.

For whatever was written in former days was written for our instruction, that through endurance and through the encouragement of the scriptures we might have hope.
Romans 15:4 (ESV)

What do you think the writer is referring to when he states, "whatever was written in former days"?

Why was it written?

How are we going to receive it? Is this a quick process?

What is the end benefit?

Who needs some hope? Hope is perhaps the most powerful emotion we experience. How often has hope been all you had? How blessed we are to find our hope in a Savior who will not disappoint!

Now hope does not disappoint, because the love of God has been poured out in our hearts by the Holy Spirit who was given to us.
Romans 5:5 (NKJV)

With both hands raised, I am thrilled to know that the Word of God, as I endure in it, will provide the instruction for which I am so desperate and a way to experience the deepest comfort and assurance of hope available this side of heaven.

> "The Scriptures are written for our use and benefit, as much as for those to whom they were first given. Those are most learned who are most mighty in the Scriptures." Matthew Henry
> [Matthew Henry's Concise Commentary on the Whole Bible]

And we have the scriptures at our fingertips.

Too often we flock to the most popular teachings, personalities, books, blogs, magazines, radio programs and television shows in search of what this single verse tells us we will find in the Holy Bible alone. Ironically, the Bible is the world's all-time bestseller, but we leave it on the shelf.

There have been many times when this Christian, church-going, Sunday school-trained girl has known the Bible could provide whatever instruction, comfort, encouragement or hope I needed; but I neither had the desire nor the patience to go looking. Instead, I took a short cut through a teacher or book or an advice column to find a satisfying answer. Sometimes, to be frank, those things do pacify, but they never satisfy. Human flesh and blood and the ideas conceived by human flesh and blood will always be temporary and leave you wanting more. However, friends, there is nothing more satisfying and complete than the Word of God. And I would dare to say nothing is more exciting than discovering it personally.

Until we are convinced that we desperately need the Word of God, we will continue in want.

Application:

On a scale of 1 - 10, how convinced are you that you desperately need God's Word? (Circle one)

1   2   3   4   5   6   7   8   9   10
(Not)   (Very)

On a scale of 1 - 10, how well do your life and habits reflect your conviction?

1   2   3   4   5   6   7   8   9   10
(Not)   (Very)

If you are convinced about your need for God's Word and have made the study of God's Word a routine and crucial part of your life, I tip my hat to you. I would love to share some chocolate cake and glean from your knowledge! Personally, I could not live without the scriptures and I know it. But, sometimes juggling the duties of being a wife, mother of two preschoolers and business owner brings me to my knees, begging God to forgive me for neglecting His word. My prayer is always one of repentance and then a plea for God to stir within me a hunger for His word like I have never known. He is faithful to deliver.

Will you do the same? If you are struggling, stop now and pray. Ask God to forgive you for having a nonchalant attitude toward the gift of His word and ask Him to give you a hunger you cannot resist. Lose the weak mindset and then, together, let's feast!

Write your prayer in the space below. Then, write out Romans 15:4 on a separate card or paper, post it and memorize it this week.

Day Two

God Breathed

Today we will continue our quest to grasp the value of scripture by examining one of the most well known passages on this very topic.

Open your Bible and read 2 Timothy 3:16-17 and answer the following questions.

All scripture is given by inspiration of God, and is profitable for doctrine, for reproof, for correction, for instruction in righteousness: 17 That the man of God may be perfect, thoroughly furnished unto all good works.
2 Timothy 3:16-17 (KJV)

The word translated "inspiration of God" is theopneustos. (Theos = God, pneo = "to breathe") Meaning, the words we read on the pages of our Bible are "God-breathed."

"God-breathed." "God-breathed."

Let those words sink in slowly.

What does it mean to you that scripture was given by God?

Which parts of scripture does God inspire?

If God inspired scripture, how did it end up in the hands of humans?

Read 2 Peter 1:20-21 for insight from Peter, an apostle of Jesus Christ.

I can only imagine how those men felt as the Holy Spirit moved them to speak and write with such power and conviction!

Look back at our verses in 2 Timothy, chapter 3. Please list the four things ALL of scripture provides (vs.16)
1)
2)
3)
4)

Commentator Warren Wiersbe describes each of the four things so helpfully. I have simplified his commentary here:

Doctrine = what is right.
Reproof = what is not right.
Correction = how to get it right.
Instruction in righteousness = how to keep it right.

So, as we study the Bible we are able to learn and identify what is right, what is not right, how we can get it right and how we can keep it right. How profound! Several years ago when I first grasped the wholeness of this verse, I was amazed by God's superior wisdom in covering us. Everything we need to know exists in the pages of His word. Only God could manage such a thing.

I believe God is going to reveal some powerful truths to us as we dig into His word in the days ahead.

***Take time to write down a few things for which you need to find clarity. Is there something you need to determine as being right or wrong? Is there something you need to know how to correct? Be specific. You'll be returning to this question later in the study.**

Now, re-focus on verse 17. What reason are we given as to *why* we have access to ALL of scripture? (17a)

The word translated "furnished" or often, "equipped" is from the Greek word *exartizo* meaning "to fit out, to prepare perfectly, to complete for a special purpose."

My husband loves to tinker and invent new things. His most recent project has had him searching all over the Internet and in hardware stores for a very specific clamp. After several failed attempts, he decided to create a mold. Once the metal is in the mold, he applies tremendous pressure, *first* to remove what is unnecessary, and *second* to transform the metal into the right shape. The finished product is one that has been furnished — perfectly — for his purpose. It is the same idea used here.

We, "by means of the scriptures," are being fitted for spiritual service. God uses His word to mold us into whom He desires us to be for His purpose

Can you name an area of weakness or incompleteness that you know God would like to remove or transform in you?

I can name several. Unless you are already perfect or complete, you need the word of God to change you. Far too many people try to change on their own. It never works. Change is temporary unless the power of God, through His word is your source. I love the teachings of Paul, a bondservant of Jesus Christ. In Romans 12 he teaches us the personal responsibility we have to live out our faith. The first part of verse 2 says,

And do not be conformed to this world, but be transformed by the renewing of your mind...

My prayer is you will make the connections between a desperate hunger for God's word, a mindset as you study it and a radical transformation. I believe the three go hand-in-hand. This is why this first week of establishing our minds is so important. God wants to make us complete, ready and fully equipped to do His work. The Bible is our training manual. And the best news is that through Christ, we can change. As Paul also teaches in chapter 5 of 2 Corinthians, it is God's desire we become new.

Read 2 Corinthians 5:17.

Read Ephesians 3:14-21. It is because of Christ, through His power and with the knowledge of His love that we are filled with the fullness of God.

The Word of God transforms.

Application:

The first step in gaining a proper mindset and a willingness to transform is to recognize who God is as revealed in His word. Once we catch a glimpse of who God is, we are more likely to grasp what He has accomplished through Christ on the cross. Then, we realize we must repent. Allow this verse to speak to you.

Repent therefore and be converted, that your sins may be blotted out, so that times of refreshing may come from the presence of the Lord,
Acts 3:19

List any sins you need to confess and forsake.

I believe the next step is to remember the work God is doing and to be renewed in spirit.

Examine Ephesians 3:8-21 and meditate on the work God is doing in your life right now, in this season. Identify and write down three specific areas or ways you see Him at work.

1)

2)

3)

Now, finish today by soaking in three short verses; Philippians 1:6, 1 Thessalonians 5:24 and 1 Corinthians 1:9. Praise Him for His faithfulness!

Don't forget...
You can get fun group study tips and activities at jaclynrowe.com.

Day Three

Handle the Word

I hope yesterday was a time of refreshing for you. It is always cleansing to go before the Lord in prayer with an attitude of repentance and a desire to learn from His word. I cannot help but think of **1 John 1:9** which says,

If we confess our sins, He is faithful and just to forgive us our sins and to cleanse us from all unrighteousness. (NKJV)

Deep breath. Thank you, Lord.

I hope we have established the value of scripture, the completeness of scripture and our desperate need for it as Christians. Before the week ends, we will examine what Jesus himself had to say about God's word. But for today, our focus is on how we should handle God's word.

What should we do with the Holy Bible? Should we merely thank God for it, hang verses on our walls, display a pretty Bible in our homes, honor it by standing when our pastors read it and make sure we speak up when politicians try to ban it? Well, yes. Perhaps we should or could do all of those things. However, the Bible itself gives us instruction.

As I am writing this, the very first verse that pops into my mind is **2 Timothy 2:15.**

Study to show thyself approved unto God, a workman that needeth not to be ashamed, rightly dividing the word of truth. (KJV)

My husband, Nathan, and I have served in various roles in the AWANA program at our church. We have been serving together since our church began the program several years ago. 2 Timothy 2:15 is the theme verse.

I remember teaching this verse to young children. "Study" they seemed to understand. "Approved unto God" they seemed to get. The rest of the verse? Forget it. I remember being asked, "what is a workman" and "what does 'rightly dividing' mean?" I remember saying "a workman is someone who is doing God's work or serving Him." And then I remember the heaviness I felt personally as I explained the final portion of the verse. I explained to the young boy that the verse meant we should study and know God's word fully, enough to handle it well. I also insisted our need to be able to share it with others in a way that would make God smile, explaining that we should never have to feel ashamed for not knowing His word. Rather, we should study hard.

Sigh.

The conviction was strong. Still is. We need to "handle" God's word well. Recently, this verse has come back to center stage for me. My younger brother has been studying and teaching apologetics at our church. He and I have discussed this verse at great length. Apparently, there was more God wanted me to grasp from this teaching.

The word translated "study" is *spoudazo* and is the verb related to the word *spoude* which means "earnestness or zeal" often translated "be diligent". Further research shows that the idea being stressed by the author is that we should study as if we are going to be tested or put on trial, literally "to be bent upon."

Perhaps it will best sink in this way: we are NOT to casually read the Bible. We are NOT to think or assume or excuse or guess or, heaven forbid, make-up things concerning what the Bible says or does not say. We are to study.

There are so many verses that compliment this one. Let's drive this home with a few.

Read Proverbs 2:1-5, highlighting or circling the word "if" as you go. As you work through the rest of the study this week, continue noticing how often the word "if" is used.

Why do you think the writer keeps using the word "if?"

In verse 4, to what is the word of God compared?

What will we come to understand "if" we *receive, treasure, incline, apply, cry out, lift up, seek* and *search*?

Our Father God is not going to force His word on us. We have a decision to make, a mindset to establish, in regard to His word and this one word — if.

Look up Psalm 119:97.

Could that verse be written about you? Could you pray that verse and have it be true of you? I pray it is. Oh, how I struggle to make it a reality in my own life. How quickly my zeal for scripture can fade when I neglect obedience. However, when you are obedient to the call...no, rather *the command*...to study, are you ever disappointed? Neither am I. Convicted, yes. Disappointed, discouraged, less joyful? No. Here is why:

Blessed are the undefiled in the way, who walk in the law of the Lord. Blessed are they that keep his testimonies, and that seek him with the whole heart. (KJV)
Psalm 119:1-2

Here is the point for today, simply put: study hard.

Application:

If this can apply, please list below your three best excuses for hardly studying the Bible. Take a minute to really think this through with complete honesty. God already knows. Perhaps you've never made yourself aware. Do you have children? Are they still babies and you're sleep deprived? Do you work long hours? Do you spend all of your "spiritual hours" serving? Do you dislike reading? Do you feel you know God's word well enough? Do you think you are not smart enough to get it anyway? Do you simply enjoy television more? Are you addicted to social media or another Internet site? Go ahead, make your list.

1)

2)

3)

Now, through prayer, tell God your reasons and ask Him to reveal the truth to you.

I know it's not always easy to make the time. I get it. But, the truth is we have no excuse. We are so ridiculously blessed in our American culture. The Bible is available to us in more formats than we can list, more commentaries than we can read, more study-help books than we can afford. We can read, listen to, or watch the Bible any time, anywhere.

The truth is, you and I have as much of God as we want to have.

No more excuses. Just study hard.

I encourage you to fall asleep tonight reading Psalm 119.

Day Four

Jesus is the Word

In the beginning was the Word,
and the Word was with God,
and the Word was God.
2 He was in the beginning with God. 3 All things were made through Him, and without
Him nothing was made that was made...
...14 And the Word became flesh and dwelt among us, and we beheld His glory, the glory
as of the only begotten of the Father, full of grace and truth.
John 1:1-3, 1:14

Focus on the phrase, "and the Word became flesh." Who is John describing for us?

Focus on the phrase, "and the Word was God." Again, whom is John describing for us?

When we study the Bible it is imperative that we understand we are equally studying Jesus. Now, I am no Bible scholar, but when I break this down here is what I conclude: Jesus on earth was both God in the flesh and the Word of God revealed in the flesh. When we study the Bible, Jesus is who we are after. Even in the story of an Old Testament king, we will zero in on God. What we will learn about *Him*, His character and His ways is what should motivate us.

As the great American Christian pastor and author A.W. Tozer said, "What comes into our minds when we think about God is the most important thing about us."
[Snyder, John. *Behold Your God, Rethinking God Biblically*. Mississippi: Media Gratiae, 2013.]

As we study the Word, our search is not for ourselves, but for God. Our goal is to learn Him.

Throughout the book of John, Jesus teaches us who He is, claiming to be everything from the Messiah and the Christ to the bread of life to the light of the world to the door to the good shepherd and more. But, perhaps one of His most familiar and profound claims is made in the following verse.

Read John 14:6 and fill in the blanks.

Jesus said to him, "I am the _____, the _____ and the _____. ____ ____
comes to the Father except _____ me."

For our purposes this week, I'd like to focus on the fact that Jesus said, "I am the truth." So, if Jesus is the Word and Jesus is the truth, then the Word is true and

Truth is a person! If A = B and B = C, then A = C! Right? We can trust Him. We can depend on His word. We can live by it and as we do, it will sanctify us.

The world we live in does not recognize the truth. Living in the technology age is making it difficult to decipher fact from fiction. There is not a single topic we can't research and have thousands of theories on in a matter of seconds. As my younger brother says, "our generation knows *too* much."

How can we determine truth?

How can we be certain that what we are holding on to is real?

Read John 8:31-32 and reconsider the questions above.

Then Jesus said to those Jews who believed Him, "If you abide in My word, you are my disciples indeed. And you shall know the truth, and the truth shall make you free."
John 8:31-32

The result of knowing truth is freedom. How many people do you know who are living in bondage? They live paralyzed by confusion, frustration, dependency, addiction and survival, jumping from one bandwagon to the next. May I suggest to you that they live in such a way because they have not experienced the FREEDOM found only in truth.

Even more so, we can conclude, because Jesus was speaking here to Jewish believers, it is possible many of us have not experienced the fullness of the freedom Christ offers. Why? We choose to *sample* His word, but not to *abide* in it.

I took the liberty to look up the word "abide" in Vine's Complete Expository Dictionary where I discovered the word translated in John 8:31 means "to continue." If we are "to continue" in Christ's word, then freedom becomes a process. We don't come to know truth and freedom in one solitary dose. We must remain in it. Perhaps that is why Paul told us in 2 Timothy to be diligent and in Romans that "through endurance" we might have hope.

Let me encourage you to keep on keeping on. As a teenager at a youth conference — you know one of those loud, stay up all night, go crazy, check-out-all-the-cute-boys events — I was challenged to select a "life verse." Yes, youth conferences can have a profound impact. We were to memorize and meditate on that verse so that we would always have a "go-to" in times of discouragement. I am convinced the Lord gave me Galatians 6:9 well over a decade ago. If I had a cent for every time this verse has brought peace and patience to my weary soul, I'd have...well...at least a few dollars!

*And let us not grow weary while doing good, for in due season we shall reap **if** we do not lose heart.*
Galatians 6:9 (NKJV) *emphasis mine*

Of course, there is that word "if" again. So much depends on our choices, doesn't it?!

Not only was Jesus God in the flesh and the Word of God revealed in the flesh, He knew and He applied the scriptures.

Read Matthew 4:1-11 and answer the following questions.
Where is Jesus and what are the circumstances in this passage?

How does Jesus respond to the devil's temptation?

How much of God's word does Jesus say we need to live by? (vs. 4)

Look up Deuteronomy 8:3.
This is the scripture Jesus was referring to when He said, "It is written."

Why did God allow His people to go hungry in the wilderness in the first place? (see Deut. 8:2-3)

The Israelites failed often when they were tested. Jesus did not. Through the use of God's word, He did not stop being hungry, but He did stop the devil from pursuing Him further.

Then Jesus said to him, "Away with you, Satan! For it is written, 'You shall worship the Lord your God, and Him only you shall serve." 11 Then the devil left Him, and behold, angels came and ministered to Him.
Matthew 4:10-11

Funny how Satan reacts when you start quoting him scripture! It was true for Christ and it is true for us. The key, again, is to know the scriptures first.

So, before I give you the main point today, let's review what we have established so far:

- **Until we are convinced that we desperately need the Word of God, we will continue in want.**
- **The Word of God transforms.**
- **Study hard.**

And for today:

By the example of Jesus and because of Jesus, *continue* in the Word.

Application:

Go back to day two, page 13, and locate *ONE* thing you wrote down when I asked you to name some things for which you need clarity.

On the left side of the chart below, list as many words as you can think of that relate to your chosen topic. (You may need more space.)

Next, look up each of the words in the concordance/dictionary or topical index of your Bible and record the corresponding verses on the right side of the chart.

As time permits and your desire prompts, look up the scripture. Once you find a verse that speaks truth to you, write it out, memorize it and apply it when you are tempted to think wrongly.

TOPIC	SCRIPTURES

FOR EXAMPLE:

I need clarity on how to have a Godly home.

TOPIC	SCRIPTURES
wife	Gen. 2:24, Prov. 18:22, 19:14, 1 Tim. 3:11, Eph. 5:22,33
husband	Eph. 5:22-33, 1 Pet. 3:7, Titus 2:6
family	Gen. 5:3-5, 12:3, 26:7-11, 27:33-37, Ex. 10:2, Jos. 4:21-22, Ex. 34:7, Deut. 12:12,18, Judges 8:31, Psalm 128:1, Prov. 11:29, 2 Tim. 1:5
marriage	Matt. 5:32, 19:10, 22:30, 1 Cor. 7:9, 1 Cor. 7:33, 1 Tim. 4:3, Heb. 13:4, Rev. 19:9

Day Five

Searching for Truth

As we bring the week to a close, I pray you have been refreshed by God's Word and feel a sense of renewal and zeal for studying it. I believe that as we begin to study the account of King Hezekiah, God will speak to you and hope will soar.

As a review, here are the keys to establishing a solid mindset for the remainder of this study:

Don't forget...
You can get fun group study tips and activities at jaclynrowe.com.

- **We desperately need the Word of God.**
- **The Word of God transforms.**
- **Study hard.**
- **Continue in the Word.**

A few years ago, I was reading through the book of Isaiah when God literally stopped my reading at chapter 36. Perhaps it was the change in literary structure that caught my attention or just the drama of the narrative, but my focus seemed to freeze on that chapter. I attempted several times to move on, continue with the book, but each time I was drawn back to read it again.

As I read the account, it just seemed to leap off the page. My imagination ran wild and I was locked in and dead set on understanding the story of this king. Please understand that I have been in church and a faithful Sunday school student and Bible study regular my entire life, but I was strangely unfamiliar with the name Hezekiah. After several weeks of reading Isaiah's warnings about God's judgment of sin, the story caught me off guard. Immediately my pen went to the margins of my Bible pages and God began forming in me the study you hold in your hands. How exciting to look back at how far God has brought me through the record of one man! Over time, my curiosity concerning this king took me on a journey through many pages of scripture and the Holy Spirit has taught me so much about the God I serve. My only desire is to share it with you, that God may be glorified through the study of His word.

Turn in your Bible to Isaiah 36 and read the 22 verses that set the stage for the weeks ahead; then answer the following questions.

Summarize the circumstances described in this story.

How do you think the people of Jerusalem felt as they witnessed the events described?

What do you think you would have recommended that the King do in response to the enemy's threats?

In the coming days, we will study this part of the story more in depth, but for now, please note a few things.

- This story takes place in the fourteenth year of King Hezekiah's reign. So, we will need to uncover what happened prior to this one day in history.
- King Hezekiah has some serious decisions to make concerning how to handle his enemy. So do we.
- The people under King Hezekiah's authority had to decide whom to believe and had to determine what was the truth.

Why do you think it is so hard for people to accept or find or recognize the truth in difficult situations?

The longer I live in this world and in our American culture, the more I see truth under attack. I don't mean truth only in the sense of deciding whether something is true or false; I mean in the sense of does "truth" even exist? In our post-modern culture, the very idea that there even *is* truth is being questioned. I will not take the time to go into a lecture on post-modernism — although understanding the culture around us is an important part of effective ministry (see an example from Paul's ministry in 1 Corinthians 9:19-23) — but, if you are interested you can find relevant information and a host of resources at www.bethinking.org.

The point I want to make to you is this: We are responsible for proclaiming truth.

May we refuse to sit back, cross our arms and say, "this generation is not my problem." Nowhere in scripture do I see God giving us a pass to give up and walk away. Yes, we are to be spiritually sanctified or set apart, but that is a far cry from being physically isolated and apathetic. Sanctification is for the very purpose of revealing God. Jesus commanded us to be the salt of the earth and the light of the world! It is a hard calling now, just as it was hard then.

My brethren, take the prophets, who spoke in the name of the Lord as an example of suffering and patience. Indeed we count them blessed who endure.
James 5:10-11a

Can you imagine being a prophet, or one who delivered God's message to the people, only to be often laughed at, persecuted and ignored? I so admire the strength and perseverance of the great prophets who were adamant that the truth was told. It was never their responsibility to be heard. It was their responsibility to be obedient and to proclaim the message God had given them. I believe as Christians who hold the truth in our hands we have the responsibility to get out and share it.

Read 2 Peter 1:12-21

Peter was convinced of the truth and he did everything he could to remind others of it and to ensure that, even after his death, God's truth would continue to spread.

What would it be like to have the boldness and ambition of Peter?

Read 2 Peter 2:1-2

Peter was quick to warn his disciples that there would be false teachers. There are liars among us, who would then and who will now manipulate and speak evil.

However, if you read the rest of 2 Peter, chapter 2 you will rejoice that righteousness prevails. God spares the righteous and upholds truth. Hang on to that revelation of God's character as we study King Hezekiah.

Now, back to the story in Isaiah 36...

You may have noticed on this particular day in history, the enemy of God's people had come to town and just like our enemy, he began doing what the enemy always does — he starts lying.

The enemy is a liar.

So, the questions for the people of Jerusalem and for you and I become these:

Who are we going to believe?
How are we going to know the truth?

In the study of King Hezekiah we will spend an entire week examining the lies of the enemy. You will be astounded by the relevance.

Next week, we are going to get more familiar with King Hezekiah. The summaries of his reign are recorded in 2 Kings, 2 Chronicles and Isaiah if you'd like to read ahead.

Application:

Read the summary of King Hezekiah's reign in 2 Kings 18:1-7 and write down a few things that stand out to you below.

WEEK 2 – Establishing a Context

Day One

Family Ties, Part 1

Welcome back! Our goal this week is to set the stage by gathering any information we can about what was happening in and around Judah before King Hezekiah took the throne.

Please read or review 2 Kings 18:1-7, answer the following questions, and then we will take a closer look at each answer.

Hezekiah becomes king of what nation?

Who was Hezekiah's father?

How old is Hezekiah when he takes the throne? How long does he reign? How old was he at the end of his reign? (You'll have to do the math.)

Who were Hezekiah's mother and maternal grandfather?

Now that we have established the basics, let's talk about the state of the nation of Judah. You may have noticed in verse one that Israel also had a King; Hoshea. At this time in history, God's chosen people were divided into two kingdoms, the northern kingdom of Israel (also called Ephraim) and the southern kingdom of Judah. The capital city of Israel at this time was Samaria and the capital city of Judah was Jerusalem.

Take a moment to look at the map provided in the back of this workbook. If you have a map in the commentary section of your Bible or in the back, you may look there as well. Please note the close proximity of the two capital cities. The actions of one nation had impact on the other. Often in the accounts recorded in 2 Kings, we see God's judgment applied to both nations. (See 2 Kings 17:13,19) God's chosen people were present in both groups.

To give a little background, remember God's chosen people, called Israel, were grouped into twelve tribes. The father of those twelve tribes, or sons, was Jacob (also called Israel). Jacob was the third in the Abrahamic line of God's plan. God had promised to make a great nation for Abram (Abraham). Abraham's son Isaac was the father of Jacob.

In 930 BC, Israel was divided into the northern kingdom of ten tribes and the southern kingdom of two tribes: Judah and Benjamin. Each had its' own long line of kings who put it on a roller coaster ride of righteousness and rebellion. It is through

Judah that the Messiah would come. And it is Judah that will occupy the majority of our focus. Looking at a map, you will notice Judah and Israel are smack dab in the middle of two world powers, Egypt and Assyria, making them hot property and important ground for trade.

Let's talk about Egypt. **Please list from memory anything you can recall about Egypt and its place in Biblical history.**

If you listed things like Pharaoh, Moses, slavery, the parting of the Red Sea or The Exodus you are on the right track. Egypt was located to the southwest of Judah.

Now, let's talk about Assyria. The capital city of Assyria was Nineveh and is located to the northeast of Judah. Does Nineveh ring any bells? **If so, please write down what you know about Nineveh below.**

Around 785 BC, seventy years before Hezekiah becomes King, God asked one of his prophets named Jonah to go to Nineveh.

Please read Jonah 1:1-2. How is Nineveh described?

I have to show you something I find humorous that really has nothing to do with Hezekiah, but was one of those moments in Bible study that made me smile. **Please look up Genesis 10:8-11. What was the name of the mighty hunter who founded Nineveh?**

Do you not find that a little funny? If you don't know, nimrod means "hunter" in ancient times. In modern times, nimrod is slang for "idiot." I leave it up to you to determine how the word has shifted from hunter to idiot. If only I could share this discovery on an episode of Duck Dynasty! Too funny.

Anyway, hundreds of years later when Hezekiah takes the throne, Nineveh is still evil. Without getting carried away in Jonah, Nineveh's repentance and newfound mercy must not have lasted too long because by Hezekiah's day they weren't only evil, they were in control. Judah and Israel alike are being controlled and occupied by Assyrians when Hezekiah takes the throne.

Let's take a partial look at how this happened.

Remembering that Hezekiah's father was Ahaz, read 2 Chronicles 28:1, 5-8 and 28:16-18. What happened to Judah under Ahaz's watch?

How is Hezekiah's father described in 2 Chronicles 28:1-4?

Read 2 Chronicles 28:19 and explain who you think was responsible for Judah's bad position and why?

I want to stop right here, pull you away from history and challenge you to make application.

Application:

Please fast forward one generation and read 2 Chronicles 29:2. Write down how King Hezekiah is described.

How do the descriptions of Ahaz and his son, Hezekiah, differ?

Here is the point I want to make: You do not have to do as your father has done. You have a choice.

Hezekiah could have easily continued in his earthly father's footsteps. He could have continued to worship false gods and been greedy, foolish and rebellious. It was what he had grown up around. But, scripture describes two very different characters in Ahaz and Hezekiah.

Some of you have been blessed by a loving, Godly example in an earthly father and should be grateful. But for others, your earthly father has been or was nothing but a disappointment. Your father is or was nothing like Christ. Do you feel the hope scripture offers in Hezekiah?

Our God can turn things around. Think about the possibilities.

Here are personal questions that require time and deep thought. Are you following in ungodly footsteps marked out by your earthly father? List any area you struggle with that seems to be a "family thing" and ask God to help you see the link between generational habits and sin.

Day Two

Family Ties, Part 2

Family roots run deep. It is not always simple to sort through all the questions and even harder to establish adequate answers. But, I do think it is beneficial and crucial to think deeply about how our family trees affect us. We will spend today drawing a few conclusions from Hezekiah's family ties to help us best understand his frame of mind and experiences as he takes the throne. Like Hezekiah, you and I must deal with the fact that our parent's actions and inactions have affected us and the roots run deep.

Let's briefly look back one more generation to Ahaz's father and Hezekiah's grandpa, Jotham.

Please read 2 Chronicles 27:2 and 2 Kings 15:34-35 and see if you can fill in the blank below.

Ahaz's rebellion began with the c _ m p _ _ _ is _ _ g character of his father, Jotham.

Is it possible King Jotham's neglect to correct his people made room for Ahaz to be drawn into a life of sin? I think so. Notice in those passages, Jotham had good intentions. He was a "good" person. At first, he is described as doing right, then comes the "BUT" or "HOWEVER". He lacked follow-through as a king and as a parent.

In your family, can you see how compromise, a lack of follow-through and neglecting the things of God can quickly unravel righteousness and lead to destruction? What a warning to us all! This leads to the point I want to make today.

Your decisions and your worship as a parent will affect the lives of your children.

Are you doing what is right in the sight of the Lord? Would the author of your life story need to add, BUT or HOWEVER in order to accurately describe your faithfulness to God? Are you setting a solid, God-centered example for your children or are you leaving room for compromise? As the mother of two young children, those questions are ever before me. I am so thankful for a Godly husband who reminds me that the most powerful lesson is in living out what we claim to believe.

If you are done raising children, may I challenge you to consider something else? You still have impact. Perhaps you have regrets to address with your children so they do not make the same mistakes, or perhaps you can offer valuable wisdom. I believe it is God's will to use *you* to teach the next generation to be Godly parents.

We need you! See Titus 2:1-8 and follow in obedience to the role God calls older Christians to fulfill.

As a point of clarification, please look up Deuteronomy 24:16. I want to point out that God holds each of us accountable as individuals. As a parent, you are not accountable to God for the decisions of your children. And as a child, you cannot point a finger of blame at your parents. Each of us will stand before God and be held personally accountable for our choices.

Application:

I'll leave you today to ponder how your family tree has shaped your spiritual life. If you are the one in your family who has taken on the task of changing the shape of that tree, allow the coming days of study to encourage you. You are about to see a twenty-five year old take the reigns and allow God to use him to turn the tables.

Conclude today by reading 2 Kings 18:5-7 and praying over the following application questions. *Side note: Please understand these questions are very personal and not necessarily meant for open sharing if you are participating in a small group setting. Allow the Holy Spirit to guide and direct your discussion.*

When I think about when I grew up or even in my relationships now, what characteristics of my parents or grandparents stand out, both good and bad?

Are there any compromising views, actions or inactions I should avoid and be cautious of?

Are there any sins I need to forgive or forsake?

What positive characteristics should I try to emulate?

Day Three

State of the Nation

Recently, my pastor spoke of French writer Alexis de Tocqueville, who after visiting America in 1831, said this about America's greatness: "I sought for the greatness of the United States in her commodious harbors, her ample rivers, her fertile fields, and boundless forests — and it was not there. I sought for it in her rich mines, her vast world commerce, her public school system, and in her institutions of higher learning — and it was not there. I looked for it in her democratic Congress and her matchless Constitution — and it was not there. Not until I went into the churches of America and heard her pulpits flame with righteousness did I understand the secret of her genius and power. America is great because America is good, and if America ever ceases to be good, America will cease to be great!"

The state of a nation is nothing more than an enlarged perspective of the convictions of the majority of people who occupy it. The truth is that nations are made up of individuals. Until the individuals are in good shape, the nation will be a mess.

Please read 2 Chronicles 28:22-25 and 2 Kings 17:14-19. List all the ways Judah, like Israel, is messed up at this point in history.

How can we relate the state of *our* nation in the 21ˢᵗ century, to the state of this nation, Judah? What similarities do you see?

King Ahaz had made such a mess of things. Have you ever been there?

Please recall a time you found yourself in a mess you created? What do you regret?

2 Chronicles 28:22 tells us it was "in the time of his distress" that Ahaz became increasingly unfaithful to the Lord.

Are you currently in a season of distress? Do you carry a large load of responsibility? Please describe the circumstances below.

I believe in learning from others' mistakes rather than repeating them. If you are overwhelmed and stressed, be warned. You are at risk for misplacing your faith. King Ahaz carried a huge load of responsibility, and he was stressed trying to maneuver the politics of his day. Rather than seeking help from God, he sought help from another king — maybe worse, a king who did not share the values of his nation. We must be so careful not to make the same mistake.

Application:

2 Kings 16:7-18 describes this very significant season in King Ahaz's reign. I will keep today's lesson short, because I want you to turn there and take the time to read what happened.

The point for today is this: Our help *must* come from the Lord, the King of kings.

Turn to Him. Place your faith in Him. My brother used the following example in a recent sermon...

Imagine you are on the edge of a cliff. You slip. You begin to fall. Would it be better to have a tremendous amount of faith in a small sapling growing out from the cliff wall and grab on to it? Or would it be better to have a little bit of faith in a great, big well-rooted branch and grab on to it?

Sometimes, we don't need *more* faith. We simply need to remember *who* it is in that we place our faith.

We need only a little faith in a GREAT God to find our help.

I will lift up my eyes to the hills–
from whence comes my help?
My help comes from the Lord,
who made heaven and earth.
Psalm 121:1-2

Day Four

Faith Doesn't Hide

Keeping in mind the state of our own country, you may be wondering if there was any hope for Judah then, or for America now. King Ahaz had imitated altar and worship practices of another king, shut up the doors of the temple and allowed God's chosen people to worship in any way they wanted. They had become a nation who embraced any form of religious practice, worshiped false idols and were overtaken by pagan influence. They had fallen so far from the original plan God expressed for them. Sound familiar?

Just to reinforce the message here, look again at 2 Kings 16:3 and 2 Chronicles 28:3 and write down the abomination King Ahaz practiced.

Can you imagine?! Burning your own children — *children* being plural — your own flesh and blood in order to appease a god who did not even exist? I find this horrifying. In Leviticus 18:21, this so-called "god" worthy of child sacrifice is named Molech and is found other places in scripture as Baal. God had made it crystal clear these acts were abominations to Him and would bring judgment. Apparently, this, along with other wicked practices, had been going on for many years. Can you imagine how young Hezekiah must have felt as he witnessed this practice and watched his own siblings be sacrificed on a pagan altar? As a young boy, he must have been scared to death. I am absolutely mortified as I allow my imagination to take me there. How did such evil exist?

Then again, perhaps now is an acceptable time to remind you that in our nation, we sacrifice the lives of innocent children every day to the gods of self-image, women's rights, choice, convenience and pride. Of course, we practice it privately so that no one has to see the horrifying act, but nonetheless, we also allow abominations in our nation. (See Proverbs 6:16-18.)

Do you find it remarkable how we are so quick to judge Judah, but not ourselves? Surely America, "one nation under God", a Christian nation, a righteous nation will never endure God's wrath or judgment, right? We could not possibly be guilty of such idol worship...could we?

The contexts of the passages we are studying represent a wicked time in history. And we, in the 21st century, are also living in a wicked time.   But, if I think about it, I cannot recall a time in history that was not horribly wicked. Ever since sin entered the picture in the Garden of Eden, man has been wicked, rebellious and awful. It seems Judah is going to get what is coming to them. They cannot avoid captivity and destruction, and therefore it really seems all hope is lost. In fact, if you were about to take the throne of a divided kingdom of God's chosen people who were living under the control of a wicked Assyrian king, would you even want the job? Had I been in Hezekiah's position, I would have gone into hiding rather than taking that job!

My friend, for too many Christians, hiding is exactly what we've done.

Please allow me to delve into this deep concern I have for just a moment. We look at the world around us and get so discouraged by the moral filth and neglect of God's truth that we just want to batten down the hatches of our churches and wait for Christ's return.

I have heard many Christians talk as if we are living in the worst and most wicked time in all of history. They are mightily convinced Jesus will return soon to get us out of this mess.

Do not misread me. Christ's return will be the most awesome, incredible day and I pray, "Lord come quickly!"

However, my fear is that sometimes we get so caught up in our pessimism — because our focus is on the world and not on the Kingdom of Christ, which is not of *this* world — that we fail to remember our hope, the joy set before us and the victory we rightly claim. I have sat in too many Christian circles where there should have been strategizing on how to win the lost, rather than envisioning of how the "wicked" are going to feel when Jesus appears in the clouds.

God is not interested in attending the pity parties we hold to point out the sins of the world while we conveniently avoid addressing our own.

Would God have us sit down, ignore and shut out the evil around us while maintaining our pessimistic whining as we await His coming? Or, would He instead have us get up, put on the full armor of God and get in the fight to win souls for His kingdom so that when He returns we are found worthy?

We must not allow the moral bankruptcy of the world around us to paralyze our faith.

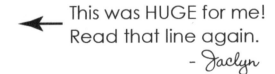
This was HUGE for me! Read that line again.
— Jaclyn

Why?

Because our God desires to reconcile the world to Himself.
Because He has already done everything necessary to heal moral bankruptcy.
Because faith that is inactive is dead.

Please read James 2:14-26.

What distinct actions in your life are direct results of your faith?

Is there not hope for America? Must we give up or must we get in the battle?
We are about to embark on a journey with a man who could have easily given up hope for his people.

But, he had bold, non-paralyzed faith.

Hezekiah, despite all he had seen and been through, believed in the God of his father David, and he was not willing to let evil have its way.

> ## Hezekiah is going to fight for the righteousness of God's kingdom.

What about you?

Application:

Look up Psalm 139:23-24 and Ephesians 6:10-20.

Close your study time today by asking God to search you and to reveal any wicked way in you. Ask Him if you are in the center of His will, doing all that He desires of you for His kingdom.

Write your prayer here...

Father, You are the creator of all things. In You, all things exist and have their being. We need You. We ask you, today, to search our hearts, search our minds and search our souls. Reveal our sinfulness. Forgive us, Father, for doubting Your purpose. Are we who you ask us to be? Show us Your plan. Show us Your Kingdom. We want to fight for You.
Lord, may Your Kingdom come. May Your will be done.
Let it be here as it is in heaven...

Day Five

True to His Word

God's judgment would come for Judah. It was part of the covenant God had made with His people. As long as the people obeyed the Law of Moses and walked in obedience to God's commands, they would be blessed and protected by Him. If they rebelled and worshiped false gods and failed to practice the law, they would experience God's wrath and judgment. Warren Wiersbe says in *The Bible Exposition Commentary*, "God's wrath is anger motivated by love, which is anguish. It's the anguish of a father who wants the best for his children, but they prefer to go their own way." God was longsuffering toward his children, but they continually rebelled against Him, so He had to discipline them. Simply put, that was the deal. God remained true to His part of the promise.

He always remains true to His word.

There are two types of promises in scripture: conditional and unconditional. The promise that the Messiah would come through the lineage of Judah was *unconditional.* God would see it through. The promise of protection, blessing and provision was *conditional.* The people had a role to fulfill. There are many examples of both types of promises throughout God's word.

Look up the following verses and determine what promise God is making. Then, determine if the promise is conditional or unconditional and explain why.

Genesis 8:21-22

  Promise:

Genesis 12:1-3

  Promise:

1 Kings 2:3-4

  Promise to David:

  How was this promise conditional?

Romans 10:9-10

Promise:

Is this promise unconditional or conditional, and how?

On and on we could look throughout scripture to see examples of God's promises. In *What Every Christian Ought to Know,* Adrian Rogers explains a fundamental principle concerning God's will. Some things God promises will occur no matter what may happen. Christ *will* return. God *will* have the victory. These promises are completely dependent on who God is and His unwavering character. This is often referred to as God's *prevailing* will. It will prevail.

Other promises in scripture are presented within the context of one huge word — *if*. God, in His love, gives us the freedom to choose what we will do in response to His invitations and commands. This freedom is referred to as God's *permissive* will. I find it easy to remember this by thinking He has given us *permission* to choose.

God's *prevailing* will guaranteed that Christ would come through the lineage of Judah as promised. Therefore, as we read the Old Testament accounts, we anticipate that a remnant of people will make it through. However, His *permissive* will allowed room for the people of Judah to fully experience the consequences of their choice to sin.

Sometimes I wonder if the Hebrew people recognized the reality of God's judgment upon them or if they were in denial over their sin. Or maybe they knew God could not deny His covenant to establish them and make them great eventually, so they pushed the limits while expecting His mercy.

I pray that I would never take advantage of the loving nature of God and choose sin over obedience. But, in shame I'll admit to you that I have.

Can you give an example of when you knowingly sinned, leaning on the goodness of God and His forgiveness to restore you on the other end? Have you acted on the mentality that says, "It is easier to ask for forgiveness than permission"?

I want you to see a couple more things from the life of King Ahaz before we look solely at Hezekiah. We can learn much from failure. One thing that is true about God that we have seen so far is that He will punish sin. God is just. He is right in His judgment. But, what I also want you to know is that Ahaz had the opportunity to turn.

Read the account Isaiah records from 734 BC when Ahaz is being threatened by Syria and Israel in Isaiah 7:1-10.

Record here the two specific verses where we are told the Lord said or the Lord spoke again on behalf of Ahaz.

Verse____ and verse ____

Fill in the blanks to record the response Ahaz gave in Isaiah 7:12 (NKJV):

"But ____ said, I ____ ____ ask, _____ ____ I test the Lord."

Notice how he tried to make telling God "no" sound spiritual. I am so good at that. I can justify just about anything. It's a talent of mine.

A couple of years ago my church was preparing for a church-wide dinner. The goal was to invite people who do not normally attend church and make them feel welcome. We were expecting around 700 folks for lunch. A sign-up sheet was passed around from class to class requesting volunteers to serve in some capacity dispensing drinks, doing dishes, clearing tables, that sort of thing. Well, I had two young children. Need I say more? I knew in my heart God desired for me to be a servant and to love people by meeting their most basic needs. I knew my help was needed. But, in case you missed it, I had two young children. I decided not to help. Easily, I felt justified in my decision by concluding that I would be a better mother by focusing all my energy and attention on them. They needed me. After all, they are only little once, right? Somebody else could surely do the work this time.

Before the event rolled around, the Lord provided a book I was reading about serving as a family. Here's your sign. I also heard that an older woman in our church was frustrated because none of the young mothers had offered to help. Guilty. Her comment was something about not using our children as an excuse to not serve the God who blessed us with them. Ouch. Ironically, God used that gossip wheel to further convict my heart. While neglecting my children was not a good option, I knew there must be a way to successfully parent and serve at the same time. So, when the day came, I recruited my two preschoolers and a large trash can on wheels. Together, we cleared tables so Daddy could help store them, and we worked until the job was done. My kids loved the experience! Rather than seeing Mommy be selfish because of them, they saw how God could use a family to serve Him. Sometimes a small thing becomes a huge lesson in obedience.

Without even knowing you, I'll bet there is some area in your life right now where you are saying "no" to God and justifying it all the way. Living in our flesh, we are just ridiculously selfish.

If you continue to read about Ahaz, you'll learn that rather than obeying God and asking for His help to spare the nation, Ahaz turns to other nations. This mistrust in God leads to the predicament we find the nation in just as Hezekiah is about to take the throne.

The point to grasp here is that God's mercy is always extended to us. We always have the opportunity to change our mind and do the right thing.

Had Ahaz listened to Isaiah and turned back to God in repentance, I know God would have shown him mercy.

Read James 2:13 and fill in the blanks.

_____ triumphs over _____.

Not only that, even in the midst of God chastening His people, we see grace woven through His character.

In Isaiah 7:3, Shear-Jashub literally means, "a remnant shall return". God had told Isaiah that the people would not listen until just about all had been lost.

But, there was always the remnant that God would see through.

His grace would remain intact and His purposes for Judah to bring forth the Messiah would be fulfilled. (See Isaiah 6:11-13)

Aren't you glad to know that God will carry out His plan? Aren't you glad to know He will be faithful to His promises? No matter how ugly the world was, or is, God is watching over His people and working to bring about His will. However, these particular Judeans were missing out on being a part of His marvelous plan.

The lunch event at my church would have gone on just fine without me. The tables would have gotten cleared and put away. But, my family would have missed the blessing of serving together and God would have been robbed of His glory through us. I pray your desire is to participate in His plan.

Application:

What blessings may you be missing because you refuse obedience and prefer your own way?

Look back at Isaiah 7:3. Later in the study, you will understand why this is important, but for now simply answer this question:

Where did the Lord tell Isaiah and his son to meet Ahaz? Be specific.

WEEK 3 – Establishing a King

Day One

A Time to Stand

Nineteen years after Ahaz's decision to tell God "no", Hezekiah, at the ripe age of twenty-five, comes on the scene as the official ruler of Judah. History implies he probably co-reigned with his father before having full power over the throne. How hard it must have been for him to submit to the authority of his father as king. Some scholars believe he served as co-regent with Ahaz for about fourteen years. What frustration!

However, he must have been preparing for the day when he could rule, because immediately he moved to action.

Read 2 Chronicles 29:1-19

Hezekiah begins living up to his name. The root of Hezekiah, sometimes translated as Ezekias, is a verb stem that means *strengthen, fortify, hold, seize, gather one's strength,* or *to take courage.* I love those three words; gather one's strength.

Describe a time in your life when you needed to "gather your strength" and how you did it.

I hope if you stand in need of strength or courage to do the right thing, you find it through God's word and the lesson of this king.

In addition, I admire Hezekiah's determination to move quickly. He doesn't waste time forming committees and asking for advice. He goes back to the fundamentals of worship and holy living and makes bold moves. The consulting would come, but only after he set the record straight.

Read 2 Chronicles 29:3. When did Hezekiah begin to turn things around and right the wrongs of his father?

There is certainly a time when we need to yield, pray and seek wise counsel, but sometimes we just need to stop making excuses and do what we already know is right. Some things really are clear. Lord, help us know the difference!

When sin is consuming the world around us, be it in our homes, schools, businesses, neighborhoods, churches or elsewhere, we should act with urgency.

Have any sinful behaviors or attitudes crept in and become acceptable in your circle of influence? Take a moment to consider each of these places and name the sin.

My home:

My family:

My church:

My neighborhood or school:

My workplace:

Read 2 Chronicles 29:4-9 and make a list of errors that needed corrected.

What had resulted because of poor leadership and sin? (vs. 9)

Sin always has a price. Never believe the lie of the enemy that says, "you're getting away with it, nothing bad is going to happen." Wrong. Sin is *always* harmful and leads to death. Refuse the lie.

Look above at the personal list of sins you named next to the categories my home, my family, my church, etc. Take time to consider the cost of each sin you named.

What is Hezekiah's desire in verse 2 Chronicles 29:10?

Hezekiah then intends to motivate the Priests and Levites to join him. Write out verse 11 in your own words here:

I love this! ➝   **"...the Lord has chosen you...."** *(vs. 11)*

Dear friends, let those words sink in deep. Long before these particular men were born, God had determined that Aaron and his sons would be set apart for His special work in the tabernacle.

Read Exodus 27:21 and 28:43.

Chosen. How easy it is to forget that long before you were born, God chose you. (Romans 8:29-30) He determined the way for you to have a relationship with Him. As marvelous and complete as that provision is, there's more. He has a purpose perfectly fitting for you. Do not be negligent now.

Application:

Personally, there is no greater motivation than when I realize God has chosen me and called me out for a specific purpose. What other push do I need?! In those moments when the voice of God is so clear, the love I feel from Him is more than reason enough to obey.

For the love of Christ compels us, because we judge thus: that if One died for all, then all died; 15 and He died for all, that those who live should live no longer for themselves, but for Him who died for them and rose again.
2 Corinthians 5:14-15

The problem is, the part of me who loves Jesus seems to be at war with the part of me who still loves...well...me. Before I knew Christ, I didn't think about what God would want. I only thought about myself. Although the Spirit of God now lives in me, I still fight the urge to be self-centered rather than God-centered. Often the cycle goes something like this: God speaks to me by way of the Holy Spirit; I am convinced of what God would have me to do to join Him in His work; I surrender in obedience and become quite excited.

Then, my old self takes over and I begin naming all the reasons it just won't work: I don't have time, I am overcommitted, I am not smart enough, I am inadequate, I have children, I can't do it as well as someone else, I don't foresee it making a difference, and the list goes on. Notice the common denominator in each phrase?

One word — *I*.

The priests and the Levites had been sinfully neglecting their work for God's kingdom. **Have *you*? What is keeping you from joining God in His work?**

Addressing sin is a fundamental step in living a life of bold faith. If you are struggling in this area, I urge you to read the book of James. It will help you examine yourself and gain wisdom as you proceed in your calling.

Day Two

A Time to Return

In yesterday's lesson we learned God had chosen the priests and Levites for a specific purpose. However, under wicked King Ahaz, they had been forbidden to perform their duties. Apparently they had resolved to accept the pagan culture around them. I do not want us to overlook the severity of Judah's situation.

To review, turn to 2 Chronicles 29:4. Who did Hezekiah summon for his first public meeting as King?

For context sake, please journey back in time to catch a glimpse of the roles the priests and Levites had been assigned in God's plan.

Read Exodus 19:3-6.

The Lord God delivered the message to Moses that He had chosen Israel. Not only did God give them an order, He did it in such a way that His presence and power were completely undeniable.

> *The people knew it was God and they were whole-heartedly in agreement with His commands.*

God follows with specific instructions for how He expected His people to live and worship Him. The people were to keep His commandments. His promises to them were conditional, based upon their willingness to obey.

Read Exodus 28:1.

Moses' brother, Aaron, and his sons for all generations were chosen to be priests. I want you to grasp that priesthood was their only option. They were not chosen to aspire to be something else. They were chosen to be priests. And they agreed to the job.

Being a priest meant they would represent the Jews before God. We know this was an enormous responsibility by reading the instructions for their garments in Exodus 28 and the instructions for the job in Exodus 29 and Leviticus 8. Under the old covenant law, the actions of the priests would allow the people to have a right relationship with God. Because sin is unacceptable in God's sight, the priests were required to make sacrificial offerings.

The blood sacrifice, offered by the priest, was the only way to appease God for sin. Without the sacrifice, the people were unacceptable to the Lord. Do you see the foreshadowing of Jesus?

It was *crucial* that priests followed the Lord's instructions for sacrifice, worship and holiness.

Priests were the only ones allowed to approach the dwelling place of God's presence, known as the Holy of Holies, located behind the veil in the temple. Priests would tie a rope around their ankle that would reach behind the veil and was long enough to still be accessible outside of it. If a priest entered the Holy of Holies in sin, God would strike him dead. Since no one else was allowed to go behind the veil, the priests' dead body would have to be dragged out by the rope.

Serious business. The responsibility bestowed upon these priests is unfathomable to me.

How do you imagine our churches would be different if our very lives depended on how we approach the presence of God, pure and without sin?

God, forgive us for reducing your holiness to ours. You are still as holy today as you were then.

Spiritually, our very lives *do* depend on how we approach the presence of God. We still must approach Him pure and without sin. This is only possible through the blood of Jesus Christ.

Praise God we can now approach the throne of grace through our High Priest, Jesus Christ! The Old Testament priests did not have that same access; rather, they demonstrated what Christ would do for us.

Never forget that every Old Testament account is ultimately aimed at the person of Jesus Christ.

Read Hebrews 7:26-28 and 9:11-12 and record your thoughts.

Now, back to the Old Testament priests. Read Numbers 3:1-4. Please list the names of Aaron's sons.

What happened to the two oldest sons? (See Leviticus 10 for more.)

Anytime we agree to what God has commanded and then rebel against it or fail to keep our commitment, we have turned our back on God and are treading on dangerous ground.

Recall King Hezekiah's first speech in 2 Chronicles 29:5-11 when he explained this concept well. Disobedience meant God's wrath had fallen on Judah and Jerusalem. Many men died and many women and children had been taken captive.

Can you imagine?

Judah was unrecognizable as a chosen nation devoted to God. As in the days of Nadab and Abihu, disobedience resulted in severe consequence.

Now, read Numbers 3:5-10. From verses 6-8, please describe the role of the Levites.

For further study on God's instruction and provision for the priests and Levites, see Numbers 8:5-19, 25-26, 35:2-3, 1 Chronicles 9:22-32 and 1 Chronicles 23:28-32. In studying these scriptures you will begin to understand the holy nature of God and that God *always* equips those He calls.

In 1 Chronicles, King David is preparing for the rebuilding of the temple, and in preparation he divides 38,000 Levite men into different roles of service. David's law was still in effect when Hezekiah takes the throne, but it had been completely disregarded.

Anytime we step away from God's plan and His appointed purpose for us, it will cost us.

With this information in mind, reconsider how Hezekiah's first summons may have taken place. He had been King for a few days when he calls the priests and the Levites together. There is no way to know for sure, but in my mind I imagine some of these men were shaking in their sandals. They must have been aware that the King had re-opened the doors of the house of the Lord, confirming that he would not be continuing in his father's footsteps. Surely some were terrified of God's wrath. Or perhaps some were relieved that they could finally return to the work they had been assigned. Either way, at that meeting in the East Square, there must have been whispers and chatter, fear and nervousness as they tried to imagine what the king would say.

As the meeting begins, Hezekiah jumps straight to the point, bringing into focus his agenda — sanctify yourselves. He reminds them of their calling. He points out the sin that had overtaken their land. He openly and clearly shares his personal intentions, and then he challenges them to take action. His approach is a great lesson on leadership. Hezekiah knows change is imminent. He knows change begins in the heart of spiritual leaders getting back to what they were originally called and chosen by God to do.

Hezekiah knows there is no hope for the people as a whole until the right people get right with God.

If we are concerned for our own nation, our first priority should be that God's people get right with Him and get back to doing what He commanded us to do.

Read Matthew 28:19-20 and write down what the Lord Jesus commanded us to do?

Why does Jesus have the right to ask this? Hebrews 10:11-14 will help you with the answer.

The book of Hebrews explains to us that the new covenant is better than the old. We no longer need a priest to be our representative before God because Jesus Christ alone became our perfect High Priest who continues in His role forever.

See Hebrews 7:22-8:2. How does this knowledge make you feel?

Hallelujah! The veil was torn and we no longer live under the old law. I am so thankful. After studying from Exodus, Leviticus and Numbers I have to admit to you that I am not sure I could have followed all those rules. The gratitude I feel for what Christ did on the cross is unexplainable. God may no longer be calling us to serve as priests and Levites, but He has asked us to spread His Kingdom, to bear His fruit and to glorify His name to all nations. The more we understand what Christ did; the more it becomes our absolute privilege and joy to serve Him.

Application:

If you were seriously focused on Christ's command in Matthew 28:19-20, how would your influence affect each of the following categories? Be specific.

My home:

My church:

My neighborhood:

My school:

My workplace:

Would it make a difference in our nation if God's people had laser sharp focus on spreading the gospel and making disciples? Why or why not?

Day Three

A Time for Cleansing

My children are messy. No sooner than I get the kitchen floor mopped does someone spill something. It happens every time. I suppose I could just leave the mess. What is the point in cleaning up spilled juice or Cheerio crumbs when I know, without a doubt, they will find their way to the floor again? The floor will never stay clean. If you are a mama reading this, you know exactly what I mean.

But, I'll bet you clean up those spills and crumbs just like I do. It would be inconceivable to think that you would just leave spilled orange juice and crumbs all over the floor. If I don't clean it up quickly, it will get on my feet and be carried to other areas of my house. Messes never stay contained in my kitchen.

Messes always need cleaned up.

My spiritual life is messy. No sooner do I get things right with God, than I sin again. It happens every time. I suppose I could just leave the mess. What is the point in asking forgiveness when I know I'll just make another mistake? I will never be perfect. If you are a Christian reading this, you know exactly what I mean.

But, I'll bet you would encourage me to repent and come clean before God again. In fact, if I don't repent quickly, that sin will get carried to other areas of my life and before I know it, I'll be truly messed up.

Our nation is a mess. What is the point in trying to influence people who will never stay right? I suppose we could just leave it alone.

Are you seeing the pattern here?

When we are in a mess, our first priority should be a cleansing.

Let's continue reading in 2 Chronicles 29, beginning today in verses 12-19.

What was the response of the Levites to the King's meeting?

How long did it take them to start? What day was it? (Vs. 17) What day did they finish?

Notice the order of their actions in verse 15. *Before* they entered the house of the Lord, they gathered their brethren and sanctified themselves. According to the definition in my *Life Application Study Bible*, sanctification means *to cleanse or set apart for sacred use — to declare or make holy.*

Literally in those days, the men ceremoniously washed themselves and their clothing as a sign of their purity before God. Through their actions they were acknowledging they had broken the law and had need of restoration before God.

Today, we are still called to sanctification. However, we accomplish it differently. The book of Romans explains we are no longer under the law of the old covenant, but rather under the law of grace through faith in Jesus Christ. To understand what Christ did for us on the cross and our role in sanctification, I would like to take a few minutes to define some big Bible words that are crucial to our learning.

1) **Election** (Romans 9:10-13): God's choice of an individual or group for a specific purpose or destiny. *God had chosen or elected the Priests and Levites to minister in His name.*

2) **Justification** (Romans 4:25, 5:18): God's act of declaring us "not guilty" for our sins. *God sees me just as if I had never sinned.*

3) **Propitiation** (Romans 3:25): The removal of God's punishment for sin (death) through the perfect sacrifice of Jesus Christ. *Jesus took my place on the cross.*

4) **Redemption** (Romans 3:24; 8:23): Jesus Christ has paid the price so we can go free. *The price of sin is death. Jesus paid the price so we may know eternal life.*

5) **Sanctification** (Romans 5:2; 15:16): Becoming more and more like Jesus Christ through the work of the Holy Spirit. *We must continue in sanctification in order to be holy and usable for God's purposes.*

6) **Glorification** (Romans 8:18, 19, 30): The ultimate state of the believer after death when he or she becomes like Christ. (1 John 3:2)

[*Life Application Study Bible: New King James Version.* Crucial Concepts in Romans, p. 2061. Illinois: Tyndale House Publishing, Inc., 1993.] ***Italics mine.***

Now, read Romans 3:21-26 and describe how the righteousness of God is obtained.

How is this different from the picture we see in 2 Chronicles?

Jesus Christ is the difference! However, what has not changed is our need for cleansing. Even if we have placed our faith in Jesus and recognize that He is our savior and redeemer, we still must walk in newness of that life. We must exercise our faith in obedience to what He has commanded.

Application:

Read Romans 6:1-4. Are you walking in newness?

As we continue reading in Romans we learn that because of Christ we are free from sin. Before Christ we are slaves to sin, unable on our own to conquer it. After we receive Christ we are free from that bondage and through obedience we become slaves to righteousness. (Romans 6:18) Only through the power of the Holy Spirit are we able to walk in righteousness. But, make no mistake; because of Him we are able! We learn step by step to walk according to the Spirit.

When we enter the house of the Lord, holiness should be in our thoughts. I don't know about you, but I have entered the house of the Lord in craziness. With two children in tow, still combing hair and wiping toothpaste off the sides of their mouths with my licked finger, I juggle a Bible and papers to copy in one hand and quarters for my children's tithe in the other. "Hurry, kids, mommy needs to get to her class!" My husband rushes them off across the gym and I rush to the copy machine. Finally settled in, I try to focus. But, I rush through our lesson and announcements and then move quickly to our corporate worship service. Rather than focusing on the words I'm singing, I gaze across the auditorium to see who made it that day and what shoes they're wearing. Well, I love shoes, people! Someone prays and I just stand quietly, missing that beautiful opportunity to pray with him or her in my spirit or to offer thanksgiving to God and to pray for what I might gain. For the next half hour I apply the sermon to someone else's life and gather my belongings to head out for lunch. Eeeek! What a waste of time. Guilty.

God help me come to your house with intent.

I have found that when I gather with His church ready to teach, ready to worship, ready to engage, ready to receive — He is waiting. He is faithful. In my mind, each week I attend a worship service is an opportunity for a holiness check. Where have I messed up? What parts of my character, attitudes and behavior do not line up with those of Christ? Please do not enter the house of the Lord with holiness as a trailing thought. If things are messy, simply come before your Savior in repentance and experience a cleansing.

Day Four

A Time for Restoration

At the king's command and with his encouragement, the priests and the Levites sanctified themselves and successfully cleansed the house of the Lord. The debris had been removed, the tables had been dusted and the precious vessels polished. The house of the Lord was ready.

Continue in 2 Chronicles 29:18-24 to see for yourself what happens next by answering the following questions.

(Vs. 18-19) What was reported to the king?

Let's record, step-by-step, the order of events that followed.

1) **(Vs. 20) What did Hezekiah do first in response to the news?**

2) **(Vs. 21-24) What took place at the house of the Lord?**

3) **(Vs. 24) Who did the King command the burnt offerings be made for? Do you find the answer interesting?**

I love the heart of this king. He was not concerned only about his throne or his particular circle of influence. His concern was for *all* of Israel. He was king of Judah. Israel had its' own king. He very easily could have kept his focus on his own, but he did not. His command confirmed to the people that their sacrifices were for a greater cause, a broader vision. The situation reminds me a bit of Abraham Lincoln and the divided nation he faced.

Hezekiah's vision was for all of Israel to be restored.

It would be easy to overlook this part, but I think it gives us something to think about. How often do I put limits on God's ability by narrowing my view? Had I been in the king's position, I am sure I would have felt it a miracle to just get a few people back on track. Surely, God would understand my dilemma and would want me to focus on a few rather than the multitudes. I am only one person after all. I mean Jesus only really reached eleven, right?

It is true Jesus spent a lot of private time with the twelve disciples. It is true He taught them intimately and trained them to be ministers of the gospel. But, let's not get off balance and use that as the standard for all of ministry.

The influence of Jesus Christ is immeasurable. He spoke to the multitudes. He was followed by the masses. He healed and touched many broken and hurting people along the way. His immediate circle included many other men and women who faithfully ministered and served Him throughout His ministry. He spent many days debating and witnessing to the Pharisees. He came to seek and to save that which was lost. He came, not for the well, but for the sick. He came to be the savior of the world, not the teacher of the few. Jesus had a broad vision.

What does 2 Peter 3:9 reveal about God's heart toward people?

A dear Bible study teacher and friend of mine put it this way, "We will never lock eyes with anyone God does not love."

Write out John 3:16-17.

The point I believe God would have me to make is that we must be careful not to put limits on what He wants to do through us. He has broad vision.

Do you think there are times when God would have you focus on a few as Jesus did at times? If so, name them specifically?

Are there circumstances in which God would have you focus on the multitudes or a broader vision?

How do you think you can know the difference?

Considering the circumstances, what impact do you think this one inclusive decision Hezekiah had on his people?

What can you learn from King Hezekiah's example in leadership?

The sacrifices made on that day were the beginning of a turned corner for Judah *and* Israel. Through the blood of the sacrifices and the attitude of their hearts, they were restored to a right relationship with God the Father. I believe the key was that Hezekiah understood what was required to bring about restored friendship with God. Reconciliation was his highest priority for all of God's chosen people. It should be ours as well.

Application:

Read Romans 5:6-11 and fill in the blanks from verse 11:

"And not only that, but we also _____ in God through our Lord Jesus Christ, through whom we have _____ received _____."

What does it mean to reconcile?

More than anything, people need to experience reconciliation. I can think of nothing better than knowing my relationship or my standing with God, which was broken because of my sin, has been restored because of the sacrifice of Christ!

Who in your life needs to be reconciled to God? Pray for them now.

On that note, restoration leads to one thing — praise.

Day Five

A Time for Praise

Yesterday's lesson ended with this statement: restoration leads to one thing — praise. So far, we have seen the leadership gathered, the house of the Lord cleansed and the sins of *all* Israel atoned for. The people are again in right standing with God. If you need a refresher before moving on, review 2 Chronicles 29:20-24.

Let's continue examining our passage.

Continue listing the order of events from yesterday, picking up at number 4.

4) Read 2 Chronicles 29:25-26. What else did the king command?

5) Do you find it interesting that verse 25 tells us the use of instruments and music was a commandment of the Lord?

6) Read verse 27. When was the music to start? When did it end? (vs.28)

Can you imagine the noise? The smell. For too long Judah's praise had been silent. I imagine the musicians had to dust cobwebs off their harps and watch dust bunnies fall out of the trumpet horns. Simultaneously, the fresh flesh of animals began to burn, mixed with the sound of clanging cymbals; the strum of harps and the stringed instruments combined with the steady climb of the singers' voices rising above the noise of the band in exuberant praise. What a scene at the house of the Lord!

7) What did King Hezekiah and those who were with him do when the offering was finished? (vs. 29-30)

The right response to restoration is to bow and to worship with gladness.

This scene makes me emotional every time I envision it. Can you see him there? He's twenty-five years old; yet, he had been waiting for years to bring about restoration for his beloved people. Years of frustration, yearning, prayer and faithfulness came together in this moment. As he looked out over the sea of people, he experienced the greatness and power of his God. The great king did the only thing he could do. He dropped to the floor and gave worship to the only one worthy. Can you see HIM there?

As the young king gathered his composure and rose to his feet, he and the other leaders shout out another command.

8) What was the command in verse 30?

Being right with God makes people happy.

So, they sang praise. Beautifully, there was no discussion about the song list, no arguing over the best lyrics or which instruments would please the most ears. The people were powerfully experiencing freedom from their sin. Their praise was uninhibited, joyful noise before the Lord because He is good and they knew it.

I wonder if they were singing Psalm 150 all over Jerusalem that day. Perhaps King Hezekiah or Azariah, the chief priest, quoted these scriptures before they began? Perhaps they sang the very words we see here…

Praise the Lord!

Praise God in the sanctuary;
Praise Him in His mighty firmament!

Praise Him for His mighty acts;
Praise Him according to His excellent greatness!

Praise Him with the sound of the trumpet;
Praise Him with the lute and the harp!
Praise Him with the timbrel and dance;
Praise Him with stringed instruments and flutes!
Praise Him with loud cymbals;
Praise Him with clashing cymbals!

Let everything that has breath praise the Lord.

Praise the Lord!

Psalm 150

Finish reading about this great revival now in verses 31-36.

Summarize what the assembly did in response to all that had happened.

What was the condition of the people who responded, given to us in verse 31?

What do you think it means to have a willing heart?

I find it compelling to point out that their hearts were not willing *until* they had repented, been cleansed, restored and responded in praise. It is *after* we experience the grace and mercy of God that we come with willing and grateful hearts. In fact, in verse 34 we learn that when the time came to offer burnt offerings, the Levites were more upright in their hearts than the priests. Could it be because they had been busy praising the Lord in song? Praise and worship focuses our heart and mind on God and opens us up to surrender before Him.

2 Chronicles 35-36 sum up the events well:

"...So the service of the house of the Lord was set in order. Then Hezekiah and all the people rejoiced that God had prepared the people, since the events took place so suddenly." *(vs. 35b-36)*

As we have studied, much took place, but it all happened fast.

God is big enough to turn things around in a hurry.

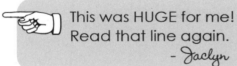

This was HUGE for me! Read that line again.
- Jaclyn

The king's action and obedience resulted in an abnormal abundance of gratitude and an atmosphere of praise. Once again, God was rightfully on the throne of His people's hearts in Judah.

Application:

There is great joy in restoration; great joy in salvation. Read and write out Psalm 135:1-3 and Psalm 144:15 here. Then honestly answer the following questions.

When is the last time you sang your heart out in Spirit-filled praise? The Lord *commands* our praise. He desires the praises of His people and He is worthy to receive it.

Do you enjoy and participate in the celebration of praise as Hezekiah commanded his people, or has your joy grown stale?

If it has been a while since you have truly experienced praise or if it is hard for you, why is that so?

Pray and ask God, as King David did, to restore the joy of your salvation. Don't wait another day to praise the Most High.

Week 4 – Returning to Obedience

Day One

Timing is Everything

It was time. The people had lived in pagan rebellion for too long. The priests and Levites had been shut out of God's house for years. The people had been under the thumb of wickedness and felt the pain of loss and captivity too often. It was time for someone to come along and take a stand. It was time for the people to return to the ways of their God. It was time for a cleansing. It was time for the remnant to be restored. It was time for some good music and shouts of praise. It was time for God to restore them to their place as His chosen people for His glory.

So, He worked through a 25-year-old King to start a revival. *It was time.*

To begin this week, I want to review how far we have come in just the first month of Hezekiah's reign. We have so much left to cover, but here is a quick recap from last week's study:

Day one:
- Hezekiah takes the throne and takes a stand.

Day two:
- Hezekiah voices the truth and calls the people to return to God.

Day three:
- In response, the spiritual leaders are sanctified and the house of the Lord is cleansed.

Day four:
- The nation's sins are atoned for, the people experience reconciliation and are restored to God.

Day five:
- Praise is on the lips of the assembly and gratitude is displayed through their actions of sacrifice and offerings. Hezekiah is happy.

We studied all this in one week and it all happened in less than four.

Now comes the hard part.

You all know what happens after a revival, don't you? People experience God at work in their lives, they make a commitment to right the wrongs and keep the right. Things are looking good! From on top of a spiritual mountain, the possibilities seem endless. God is real and nothing stands between your passion for Him and His love for you. It is a place of peace, hope and joy.

How do we maintain our exuberating awareness of God's presence? I think I can sum up in one word what must come next for revival to last. It is a word that you quickly learn after you receive Christ, experience the joy of salvation and wake up in the real world the next day. It is the word that represents everything that will test your faith and produce patience in you. This is what determines your level of spiritual maturity and your loyalty to Christ and His word.

The word is **obedience.**

Please turn in your Bible to 2 Chronicles 30 and read through verse 9.

What event had not taken place in Jerusalem for a long time?

Who did the king gather together to make decisions about the feast? (vs. 2)

It seems to me that Hezekiah had tremendous leadership qualities. He established his core — the spiritual leaders as we've read in the previous passages — first. Then, he reached out to the other leadership in Jerusalem — his counsel and princes. He knew he needed a team to accomplish what God required and he knew he needed the favor of his assembly.

As the king gathered his leadership together, what did they decide concerning the Passover? (vs. 5)

Obedience. Hezekiah knew that experiencing revival was not enough. God required more. It had been a long time since the people had taken part in the great Passover Feast. The Passover feast was a celebration that would remind them of when God's judgment passed over the Hebrew people. It was God's command to Moses that the feast took place in the first month of the Jewish calendar. However, because everything was so out of order when Hezekiah took the throne, it wasn't possible. So, Hezekiah and his leaders decided to have the feast in Jerusalem in the second month. Numbers 9:6-13 reveals a time when God made an exception for celebrating Passover in the second month due to travel or uncleanliness because of contact with a dead body. I think Hezekiah took that as a provision, a loophole in the law, for what he needed to do and was trusting in God's merciful character. His heart was right and he knew God would make an exception for him as well. In part, this decision was made so that all of Israel could be invited to attend. Although God's people were politically divided, Hezekiah's desire was for them to reunite spiritually.

I think it is safe to conclude that in this case, obedience was more important than appearance.

I love this! →

God is not after outward perfection, but inward obedience. He is after your heart.

In John 5:1-17 we read a passage where Jesus healed a man on the Sabbath, or holy day, and then told the man to "take up his bed and walk." In verse 10 the Jews scolded the healed man for breaking the law saying, "It is the Sabbath; it is not lawful for you to carry your bed." The only answer the man could give was that the man who had healed him told him to do so. The fact that he had experienced the healing power of Jesus was enough to cause him to obey.

"For this reason the Jews persecuted Jesus, and sought to kill Him, because He had done these things on the Sabbath." (verse 16)

But Jesus answered them, "My Father has been working until now, and I have been working." (verse 17)

It seems to me, God's work trumps our rules.

Had Hezekiah been more concerned with the traditions of his people rather than the glory of His God, he would have put the feast off another year and could easily have justified doing so. But Hezekiah knew God was working and he was on a mission. The mission could not wait another year. It was time.

When God is at work around you and he invites you to join Him, do it. Don't wait or justify putting it off. Do the work set before you at the time it is given. Is it time for you?

Read what happened next in 2 Chronicles 30, verse 6.

Describe the tone of the message the runners gave in all of these cities as recorded in verses 6-9.

What feedback did they receive in verse 10?

Well, well, well, isn't that just like how it happens?! You experience the greatest revival of your lifetime, grow excited, establish in your heart that you are going to carry out the commandments of your Lord and when you go and invite people to join you, you get nothing but laughed at? There is nothing new under the sun. I try to image how the runners felt. They were just the messengers, but I am sure many of them, if not all, were present at the praise service just a few days before. I'm sure they were filled with enthusiasm as they set out to share the proclamation of their country. No doubt the vision of a Passover feast was refreshing and invigorating.

But, too quickly their excitement was met with discouragement. Been there?

This makes me think of the day the disciples came to Jesus full of vigor because they had been out performing miracles and sharing the gospel. It was the day after He had healed the man by the pool as we just reviewed above. They were thrilled with what God was doing through them. Conversely, they were met with sorrow as they learned of the murder of John the Baptist. They desired time alone with their master, but the crowds swarmed and were hungry. They witnessed the miracle of Jesus feeding 5000 men and then Jesus sent them out on a boat where they endured hours, rowing in horrific winds before Jesus appeared walking on water. A day of joy quickly turned into a night of confusion. A roller coaster ride of emotion can make us question everything and tempt us to give up.

But, in all these things God is working.

Keep reading in 2 Chronicles 30:11-13.

Record the first word in verse 11 here: _____.

Nevertheless, however, even so some came. Whatever your version, the word translated at the beginning of verse 11 speaks volumes. Despite the mocking and the laughter at the king's invitation, God was working and a great multitude was headed to Jerusalem.

What was God doing in Judah in verse 12?

Application:

Write out Philippians 2:13 in your own words.

How does that verse encourage you today?

Are you discouraged or confused about what God has required of you?

How does the story we are following in Judah encourage you?

Hezekiah was following God in obedience. God was working. When we do our part, God is always faithful to do His.

Day Two

Time to Feast

King Hezekiah did not seem concerned about whether or not people would respond to his invitation to attend the Passover. His only determination was to be obedient to God and to follow in His ways. In a season of discouragement, I hope we will have the same resolve. As you read today, I think you will find great encouragement and strength in how God responds to the pure heart of his servant.

Read the events of the Passover feast in 2 Chronicles 30:14-27 then answer the following questions.

    1) What task did the gathered assembly perform first in verse 14?

    2) Why do you think the priests and the Levites were ashamed according to verse 15? Read verses 16-17 and describe the problem the priests and Levites were facing.

They had not even held a Passover feast in years and when the opportunity finally presented itself, the priests, Levites and congregation were nowhere near ready. According to the calendar, the correct month and timing had already passed and the people were totally unprepared. They had not been through the sanctification process and had come to the feast unclean. This was against the Jewish law. This was not the way it had been done before. And now the Levites had to work overtime to keep anything unclean out of the hands of the priests. This seems like a disaster. Would God even be pleased?

    3) It was against the rules of the sanctuary for the people to eat the Passover meal if they were unclean. What does verse 18 say they did?

Excuse me? This whole thing seems so out of line to me. I feel my powerful choleric, Type A personality flaring up again as I write this! If I had been in charge — and trust me, while my family tree would have kept me from being queen, I'm quite certain I would have been right in the middle of this mess — I am confident I would have lectured the crowd, highlighting their disregard for the rules and postponed the event. However, I was not in charge and, ultimately, neither was king Hezekiah.

Carefully read the next portion of the text and consider how the people responded to God by answering the questions on the next page.

4) What does Hezekiah request in verses 18-19?

5) How does God respond in verse 20?

6) How did the children of Israel respond? (verses 21,23-26)

7) How did King Hezekiah respond? (verses 22,24)

8) How did the priests and Levites respond? (verses 21,22,24-27)

9) How long had it been since all of them had experienced the mercy and goodness of God? (verse 26)

Hezekiah knew his God. He was counting on God to be faithful to unite the hearts of the people, to show them mercy and to show His glory. The mark of a great leader is one who is counting not on his or her own abilities, rules or co-workers but on the greatness and unchanging character of God!

Application:

I am so thankful for the way God works things together for our good and for His glory. God honored the pure motives of Hezekiah. It is encouraging to know that God is after the hearts of His people. His desire and priority is our relationship with Him in the midst of our circumstances, not the circumstances themselves. I find great comfort in knowing that even when things do not appear perfectly put together, God is more interested in what is being put together in my heart.

End today by reflecting on your relationship with God.

Honestly evaluate if your relationship with God is based on outward appearances or an inward relationship that results in obedience.

Spend some time writing a prayer of response to God, thanking Him for His mercy and faithfulness toward you.

Day Three

Time to Reform

The feast was over. The music had grown quiet, but the revival continued. God had shown Himself — again — to be merciful, good and real. Without doubt, the people had returned their hearts to the God of their fathers, Abraham, Isaac and Jacob.

But, the work had only just begun. They had followed in obedience by having the Passover feast, but more was needed to establish their faith in God as the one and only true God. So, before the people departed Jerusalem and headed home, they took care of one last important task.

Turn to 2 Chronicles 31 and read verse 1. What did the people of Israel do and to what extent?

They removed everything that represented devotion or worship to anything or anyone other than God Most High.

Please turn to the parallel account in 2 Kings 18 and read verse 4. What specific idol was named and how is it described?

I do not want us to miss this really interesting part of Hezekiah's reforms. One idol that was destroyed in this process was the bronze serpent that Moses had made. It is crucial that we understand where it came from to understand the impact of its destruction.

If you are not familiar, read about the bronze serpent in Numbers 21:1-9.

Nehushtan had gone from being the instrument God used to perform His ministry of salvation to an item of worship for the very people He had saved through it. Decade after decade, generation after generation, this account and the bronze-headed serpent had been passed down until eventually the people forgot the main point. They turned it into something for which it was never intended. A good and beautiful thing, given by God, had become a disgrace.

I find this profound and relevant in so many ways. I question if we are guilty of the same. Do we esteem the method of the message more than the giver of the message? God had used the bronze serpent as the thing that represented how salvation could be obtained. Years later, Jesus would come and be lifted up on a cross and we would be challenged with the same words, to look and live. But, it is imperative that we always devote our worship and apply our gratitude to the source of our salvation. May we be careful not to apply the most emphasis to our method, program, affiliation, association, building, style or anything else. Our loyalty is to God and His truth alone. This part of the story teaches us that even God-instituted things, used for His purpose, can become objects of sin. If that has become the case, I think we can follow Hezekiah's example and destroy them before they destroy us.

Application:

Is there anything in your life that you hold more closely than God alone?

Have you misplaced your affections toward a thing, even a good thing, which distracts from your worship to God alone?

What will you do to make sure God is the only one on the throne of your affections?

I'll be honest. Misplacing my affection is far too easy. "Thou shalt have no other gods before Me" is a tough commandment. The word "before" does not simply mean to give God priority on my list of gods. "Before" means "in the presence of." Thou shalt have no other gods *in the presence of* the Holy God. Since the one true God is present in all places at all times, I cannot allow my heart to have any other affections. There is no other. God is ALL. Each of us must check the altar of our heart and ask God to reveal the truth to us. I am trusting the Holy Spirit to do that very thing.

Day Four

Time to Respond

After those visiting Jerusalem returned home, Hezekiah refocused his attention on his duties as king. It was his job to establish order and see to it that his people could and would maintain their worship to God and follow in His ways. His leadership qualities continue to be on display as we read and learn about the art of delegation in the verses and chapters to come.

Please read 2 Chronicles 31:2-11.

In chapter 29, when we are first introduced to Hezekiah, we were told that he did what was right in the sight of the Lord, *according to all his father David had done.* We know David was not his biological father, but he was a father in the faith. King David was known to be a great king, a man after God's own heart. In 2 Chronicles 23:6-23 we can read about King David's plan for how the temple service would be organized. Hezekiah is following David's example. He assigns the priests and the Levites to their roles and supplies them with all they need to accomplish the task.

Next, he commanded the people to contribute support for the priests and the Levites. In other words, the men appointed to the service of the temple would not have time to work in the fields, tend sheep and provide basic needs for their families. The responsibility fell to the people to feed these men called by God to serve. This principle was carried out through the New Testament and we practice this same principle in our churches today. God uses His congregation to provide for the priests and Levites so that they can devote themselves to His word.

How did the people respond to this command? (verses 5-10)

What priority did the people place on these tithes and offerings? (verse 5)

In response to all God had done, the people gave. They did not choose to give their leftovers; they gave of their firstfruits. This means as they harvested their produce and made their products, they brought in the *first* rewards of their labor. They did not eat first, feed their families, put some back for the winter and *THEN* bring what was left. They brought a portion to the temple first. They did not bring just enough to please the king, but enough to please the Lord. They faithfully gave in abundance, laid it up in heaps and God blessed them for it. According to *Zondervan Handbook to the Bible*, the people began to give in May/June at the grain harvest and continued to the end of the fruit and vine harvests in September/October.

In verse 10, Azariah, the chief priest, explains the bounty to Hezekiah and Hezekiah has more storage rooms prepared. Verse by verse we learn how many men it took to oversee all the contributions and distribute allotments to all the cities.

Please read 2 Chronicles 31:12-18 and summarize using verse 19.

The people were relying on God to provide for them as they obediently provided for His servants. They had experienced the faithfulness of God and it compelled them to be faithful in return.

Application:

Today's lesson is short because I want you to have time to respond. I am about to ask you to answer some of the most important questions in this study. Please search your heart, mind and soul to answer honestly before God, knowing that everything is open and naked before Him. He knows your heart, loves you and longs for a deeper relationship with you. His desire is that you'll trust Him to provide as you obey His commands.

"Therefore know that the Lord your God, He is God, the faithful God who keeps covenant and mercy for a thousand generations with those who love Him and keep His commandments;"
Deuteronomy 7:9

Key question: In what ways has God been faithful to you? Name as many as you can.

Are *you* faithful in giving tithes and offerings for the work of God's church?

Do you give of the firstfruits of your labor, or do you give the leftovers?

What do you think God would have you do in response to today's study?

Day Five

Time to Realize

In a short time, Judah has come a long way. Things have certainly turned around.

Try to list from memory the main things that have changed since Hezekiah took the throne.

Once full of debris and rubbish, locked up and sealed tight, the house of the Lord has now been cleaned out and re-filled with heaps of tithes and offerings. The people have gone from idol worship and pagan influence to spirit-filled feasts and a season of praise and giving. What a difference a return to obedience makes!

Do you need to know how to turn your life around? Are you in need of a change?

When we find ourselves in a time of spiritual drought, hopelessness or frustration, we can count on the reality of obedience. God can and does turn things around when we start doing things His way. He is slow to anger and quick to show mercy. His desire is our relationship with Him. His priority is our love for Him and Him alone. His word tells us that if we love Him, we will keep His commandments. As we grow in our love for Him, we choose daily, choice by choice, to keep His word. And as we do, struggles begin to turn around. There is no shortcut to a life blessed by God. We must trust Him and obey.

A return to obedience makes all the difference.

How does this realization give you hope?

What three words are used to describe the actions of Hezekiah in 2 Chronicles 31:20?

In verse 21, how did Hezekiah approach every work he began?

What was the result?

Application:

Today, the message is simple. When we give our whole selves to seeking the Lord, He is glorified and we are blessed.

For application today, look up and write out Colossians 3:23. Memorize this verse and think of the example of King Hezekiah.

How well do you do what you do with all your heart for the glory of God?

What changes should you make in response to today's study?

but he who looks into the perfect law of liberty and continues in it, and is not a forgetful hearer but a doer of the work, this one will be blessed in what he does.
James 1:25

Week Five – Resolving to Trust

Day One

Fearing the Enemy

I remember well the first time I played indoor laser tag. It was dark...REALLY dark. I was armed and dangerous and ready to win big. Never before had I faced hand-to-hand combat and intense warfare. I had not expected to become so emotionally involved, but I did not want to die, even if it was pretend. The fear of being shot in the dark consumed me. I'll never forget the pace of my heartbeat and the way my body and mind responded to being threatened. So much so, that as I ran for my life I went full speed into a wall and nearly broke my nose! That day I experienced first hand the principle of fight or flight.

Fear is a valid and powerful emotion. Keep fear in mind as we enter this week's study.

At the end of last week we learned that Hezekiah prospered because he sought God, obeyed Him and did every work with great passion. The people of Judah were obedient and generous, and the temple ministry was in working order. Hezekiah had renewed a covenant with God and was faithfully serving Him.

Although Judah has done a major turn around, the broader picture has not changed. God's chosen people are still divided into the northern kingdom of Israel and the southern kingdom of Judah. Assyria is still the world super power. Wealthy and wicked, Assyrians occupy much of the Israeli land and are the dominant force.

Hezekiah had experienced the threat of Assyrians. Prior to taking full control over the throne, history reveals that Hezekiah co-reigned with his father, King Ahaz. The account revealed in 2 Kings gives a flash back moment I want us to learn for context sake.

Turn in your Bible to 2 Kings 18 and read verses 9-12. What happened in Israel, the northern kingdom, in the capital city of Samaria?

When did this happen?

Note: The reference to King Shalmaneser, King of Assyria and the year of Hoshea, king of Israel refer us to 2 Kings 17 when Ahaz was clearly the king of Judah. This is how we conclude that Hezekiah was co-reigning with his father during these events.

What reason does the author give for the defeat and captivity in 2 Kings 18:12?

Israel rebelled completely against God. They broke their covenant and refused to listen. 2 Kings chapter 17 gives extensive insight into the evil they practiced and why God allowed this destruction. The people were transported to Assyria and the Assyrian king brought in people from other lands to occupy Samaria. After that, a series of events transpire leaving the author to make a rather profound statement.

What does 2 Kings 17:18 say?

When we find Israel under attack in 2 Kings 18, it is partly because King Hoshea of Israel had conspired against King Shalmaneser of Assyria by attempting to team up with Egypt. They wanted to put an end to the Assyrian power streak. While Hoshea's objective was correct, his method was not. Turning to anyone but the Lord for help never pleases Him. Samaria was defeated.

God used Assyria to punish Israel. Even in their great victories, Assyria cannot take credit. God allowed his people to be disciplined for His own sake. The prophets had warned time and time again that this would happen if the people did not repent and turn back to the ways of the Lord.

Years later, the Assyrian army is next door to Judah under a new ruler, King Sennacherib. We are going to read all about Sennacherib's invasion and strategy, but first, I want us to seriously consider the position of King Hezekiah.

Hezekiah was well aware of the surrounding circumstances. He understood his enemy well. His earliest childhood memories showcased the wicked, pagan influence of the Assyrians and other heathen emigrants. He had watched how quickly the people would abandon their love for the one true God in order to pacify false gods. Located in what is now northern Iraq, the Assyrians had invaded the lands to their south and west for years. They worshiped a god called Ashur and many other gods of moon, sun, weather, love and war. The gods were unpredictable, but the Assyrians were bent on appeasing them. Assyrian leaders were power-hungry and convinced it was their right to obtain wealth at the expense of others. They demanded other nations to turn over a portion of their wealth — or else! If a nation's king did not comply, they would face a combination of invasion, slaughter and capture before their wealth would be stolen.

Hezekiah's allies in Israel, as well as his father, grandfather and many kings before them, attempted to appease the Assyrian rulers by paying an annual tribute. Of course, giving them money only made them stronger.

Given that Hezekiah had witnessed the tactics of his enemy and seen them succeed time after time, how do you think he felt?

How does it make you feel when you see your enemy attack and win time and time again?

God's chosen people feared their enemy. Fear is a powerful emotion causing one of two reactions: fight or flight. God's children had predominantly reacted in flight mode and had spent decades appeasing — rather than facing — their enemy. Israel had totally ignored God's promise of protection if they would simply remain obedient to His commands.

Can you describe a time in your life when overwhelming fear caused you to forget the promises of God?

Fast-forward to the fourteenth year of King Hezekiah's reign in 701 BC and read 2 Kings 18:13-16.

What happened first?

What did King Hezekiah do in response to the enemy's attacks?

Based on what we know about King Hezekiah and the steps he had taken to turn his nation back to God, it is incredibly disappointing to see him fall back into the habits of his father, Ahaz. He resorted to appeasing the enemy. King David did not negotiate with his enemies or try to buy them off. King David attacked and defeated them. However, fear is real and Hezekiah is human. The most powerful army on the planet just stepped into his territory and successfully took over several small cities. Hezekiah is afraid. So, in fear he not only dipped into his personal treasury to pay tribute, but also took from the temple. His goal was simple; get the enemy off his back. This event signifies a huge mistake on his part. Out of fear, he repeated the same mistake his father had made.

In response, Sennacherib draws back from Judah. But, he would return.

The enemy is never satisfied until God's people are defeated.

Application:

Do you recognize how your emotions can affect your decisions? Share an experience.

What options did Hezekiah have?

If you are currently fearful of something in your life, large or small, what options do you have for overcoming your fear?

Did you know the words "fear not" or "be not afraid" are recorded 365 times in the Bible? That is one reminder for every day of the year. God does not desire that his children live in fear, but in love.

Finish today by looking up 1 John 4:18-19.

How can you overcome fear?

Grow in the knowledge of the love of God. Only as you experience Him through a personal relationship will you learn to live in love, not fear.

Day Two

Fixing the Heart

After Judah is attacked, Hezekiah pays tribute to Sennacherib, king of Assyria, to avoid war. The Assyrians are pacified for the moment and retreat. According to scholars, the next series of significant events take place tucked somewhere between verses 13 and 14 in 2 Kings 18, verses 1 and 2 in Isaiah 36, and verses 1 and 2 in 2 Chronicles 32. It seems the authors continued to explain the political and military events before writing about what happened in Hezekiah's personal life during this time.

To study in chronological order, we will skip over to 2 Chronicles 32. First, read the summary in verses 24-26 there, and then read the parallel records in 2 Kings 20:1-11 and Isaiah 38:1-22.

(Tip: Bookmark all three books, as we will be flipping back and forth today.)

What dreadful news does the prophet Isaiah bring to King Hezekiah? (2 Kings 20:1 and Isaiah 38:1)

Perhaps you can relate to that kind of news.

How does the king react? (2 Kings 20:2-3 and Isaiah 38:2-3)

Naturally, Hezekiah is distraught. He would have only been thirty-eight or thirty-nine years old and his son Manasseh would have been seven years old. The questions loom. How would a small boy rule the kingdom if his father died? What did death even mean? Remember, the promise of eternal life was not a prominent teaching in the Old Testament culture. Jesus had not yet come. Death had not been defeated. Other than the prophets, no one talked about the resurrection of the body. In Hezekiah's day, death was thought to be the end of all life. Hezekiah was a wreck.

Turning away from everyone around him, Hezekiah prays to the only One who can save him. He claims the promise of 2 Chronicles 6:16-17, pleading with God to remember that he has been faithful and is qualified to live.

List the two major things God promises to do in response to Hezekiah's prayerful plea. (2 Kings 20:4-6 and Isaiah 38:4-6)

1)

2)

There is so much packed into these verses. The grace of God is unbelievable. Not only does God answer Hezekiah's prayer for healing by promising fifteen more years of life, he adds a promise of deliverance from Assyria for him and Jerusalem. Furthermore, He is willing to perform a miracle to prove His word. Hezekiah requests in 2 Kings 20:10 that the shadow on the sundial, or the steps of Ahaz, go backward ten degrees.

Consider this miracle. Did God's love and concern for his servant reach so far that He literally stopped the rotation of the earth for this one man?! Who, I ask you, could cause the earth to rotate backwards ten degrees but our God? Astounding! Of all the miracles in scripture, this one certainly blows my mind.

What valuable insight does 2 Chronicles 32:25 give as to the condition of Hezekiah's heart after this?

The Amplified Bible reads, "for his heart became proud at such a spectacular response to his prayer."

Do not miss an important lesson here. Answered prayer can puff us up and make us feel superior to others who suffer. We must guard our hearts even when God blesses. God had extended miraculous grace to Hezekiah and although he was grateful, (see the prayer of response he wrote in Isaiah 38:9-20) the sin of pride surfaced.

> "There is one vice of which no man in the world is free; which every one in the world loathes when he sees it in someone else; and of which hardly any people, except Christians, ever imagine that they are guilty themselves. [...] There is no fault which makes a man more unpopular, and no fault which we are more unconscious of in ourselves.[...]The vice I am talking of is Pride or Self-Conceit: and the virtue opposite to it, in Christian morals, is called Humility."
> — C.S. Lewis, *Mere Christianity*

Read 2 Chronicles 32:27-30 and describe Hezekiah's position.

What does verse 31 say God did?

Read the full accounts in 2 Kings 20:12-19 and Isaiah 39:1-2 and answer the following questions.

Who had heard of the king's sickness? What did they do?

I wish we could assume it was out of thoughtfulness and compassion that the Babylonian rulers sent a get-well card and gift to Hezekiah. The truth is, the Babylonians saw the king's illness as an opportunity to scope out territory. Under the disguise of concern, they visit the king and charm their way right into his palace. And what does Hezekiah do? He walks them right in the door and shows off his possessions — all of them.

Isaiah 39:6-7 reveals that Babylon was an enemy. God allowed the above scene to take place to test his servant Hezekiah. God wanted to reveal Hezekiah's true character so that the condition of his heart could be corrected.

Hezekiah fails this test. Isaiah lets him know the mistake he made, but in the process we see, again, the mercy of God. 2 Chronicles 32:26 tells us Hezekiah repented of his pride and once again his heart was humbled before God.

God honored his life and his kingdom. It would be another one hundred years before the Babylonian rulers would return.

Application:

Throughout scripture, God tests His people. Hezekiah was unaware and unwarned that he was being tested. He was wrapped up in the moment, enjoying the flattery of the Babylonian princes.

God needs no permission to test us.

His desire is to fix our hearts, conforming us to the image of Christ.

Here are some difficult questions to consider for application:

Are you so wrapped up in your life and your ego that you are unaware you are being tested?

How might God be testing you TODAY?

In this season of your life?

Is there looming pride in your heart, keeping you from full alignment with God's purposes?

Be sure today, your heart is aligned with the heart of God. Make a commitment to check your heart's condition daily for the glory of God.

But He knows the way that I take; When He has tested me, I shall come forth as gold.
Job 23:1

DAY THREE

Facing the Enemy

The enemy occupied Samaria, Israel. Enough time had passed for Assyria to rebuild their army and they had moved in on Judah. The small towns established just outside of Jerusalem were taken. To avoid war, Hezekiah had stripped wealth from his purse and God's house and the enemy had retreated. Hezekiah had suffered for his lack of faith and had learned to trust in God's promises.

With a grateful heart and fifteen years of promised life before him, Hezekiah reclaims the promise that God made: *He* would deliver him and Jerusalem from the hand of the king of Assyria. God would defend this city.

Hezekiah believed the promise, but he did not have any details explaining *how* God would accomplish this.

Have you ever been discouraged by the lack of details God gives?

What do you think we should do while we are waiting for God to fulfill His promises?

Let's go back to the account in 2 Chronicles to see what Hezekiah would do.

Please read 2 Chronicles 32:1-8.

After the attacks on the fenced cities, or the cities around Jerusalem, what did Hezekiah realize? (verse 2)

Scholars suppose that it is after this realization that Hezekiah pays off Sennacherib and becomes ill. Fast-forward through the illness and the visit from the Babylonians and we see a king in total preparation mode. He will be ready when the enemy comes.

Please list from verses 3-8 the six things Hezekiah did.

1.
2.
3.
4.
5.
6.

As soon as Hezekiah realized the enemy was on the move, he went to work. He called his leadership together and outlined a strategy to defend Jerusalem. At the top of the list was an idea to shut off the water flow so that the enemy invaders would not have access to a water supply. This was no easy task. Historically this tunnel is often referred to as Hezekiah's Conduit and was over 1700 feet long, stretching from the Spring of Gihon to the Pool of Shiloam. This tunnel runs around the southeastern part of the city and is a popular tourist attraction to this day.

According to Zondervan, in 1880 a boy who had been bathing in the Pool of Shiloam found an inscription telling the story of how the men who were digging the tunnel finally met in the middle, ax to ax. It is amazing to think about the amount of time and effort it took. Great pictures of the tunnel can be found online by searching "Hezekiah's Tunnel." This aqueduct also secured a water supply for Jerusalem, should they come under siege and need to lock down their gates.

Speaking of gates, Hezekiah ordered all broken down walls and the Millo structure (a terraced stone brace against the wall) be repaired and a second wall built around the city. He also made sure they would have weapons by having arrows and shields made "in abundance." He organized captains for war and called all the people together to give them a serious pep talk.

Read again verses 7-8 and summarize in your own words what Hezekiah told his people.

Hezekiah sounds much like Moses did when he encouraged Joshua in Deuteronomy 31:6, and like Joshua when he encouraged his captains in Joshua 10:25.

The clear message: be strong and courageous; do not be afraid because the Lord will do the fighting for us.

No doubt the enemy was coming. Hezekiah could have panicked, gone into hiding, demanded his people turn over their wealth or called for an evacuation. Instead, he trusted in the name of the Lord God and prepared for a fight.

I believe we must do the same.

Application:

No doubt our enemy is coming. He is on the prowl, seeking whom he may devour. We have the same options. We can panic. We can hide. We can demand someone else do something. We can run. Or, we can trust in the name of the Lord our God and prepare to fight.

In wisdom, Hezekiah considered his enemies' game plan and went on defense.

How do you think Satan might attack you or develop a negative stronghold in your life?

In what ways are you vulnerable?

Read Ephesians 6:10-20 and write down all the things we can do to prepare for battle. If you are unsure about what something means, take extra time to read commentaries and look up the cross-referenced verses. These verses are generally listed in the center or side margin of your Bible.

It is crucial we know how to face the enemy! I challenge you to share what you have learned with someone who is struggling in the battle.

If you are currently under attack, you probably feel the enemy closing in on your heart, mind and body. Tomorrow's lesson will be such an encouragement to you. Be strong, friend. God has not left us defenseless. His word gives instruction on how to face the enemy and WIN.

Yet in all these things we are more than conquerors through Him who loved us.
Romans 8:37

Day Four

Fighting the Enemy

It is one thing to prepare for an enemy that is still at bay. It is a whole different animal to square off face-to-face. What I hope we learned yesterday is that we have a responsibility to be prepared. Yes, God will defend us. Yes, God will provide a way of escape, but we must be ready. We should never be caught off guard by the attacks of Satan. Scripture informs us that in this world we will have trouble and we will face temptation. Our job in the meantime is to prepare.

Hezekiah did not sit back in the palace, waiting for God to do all the work. He took action rooted in faith.

The next portion of our text is actually where I began this journey and where I asked you to read back in week one. I was reading through the book of Isaiah nearly four years ago when I froze at chapter 36. It was this chapter that persuaded me to study all three accounts of Hezekiah. I believe the most detailed perspective of this specific event, also in the fourteenth year of Hezekiah's reign, is given in the book of Isaiah.

Please turn to Isaiah 36 and read verses 2 through 22 and answer the following questions.

Who sent whom to Jerusalem?

Who was with Rabshakeh? (see 2 Kings 18:17 as well)

"Rabshakeh" is a title describing a field commander or general. In this case, he was to function as an ambassador for the Assyrian King. Alongside him were the Tartan, or supreme commander, and the Rabsaris, meaning chief officer. In modern terms, it would be the equivalent of sending the vice president, secretary of state and top ranking general of our military to speak on behalf of the president. The Assyrian King sent them to town with a portion of the Assyrian army in tow and with one message in mind.

It is the same message our enemy attempts to employ today — convince the people they cannot be saved.

Where is the Assyrian King, Sennacherib, and what is he doing during this event? (see the parallel account in 2 Chronicles 32:9)

According to scholars, around forty-four cities had already been defeated and Sennacherib had set up headquarters in Lachish, about thirty miles to the southwest, to prepare for a conquest in Jerusalem.

Name the three people Hezekiah sends to meet Rabshakeh and list their job roles?

1)
2)
3)

Where do they meet? (see verse 2)

Stop right here. Let me get this straight. An army rides in to town following three top commanders. Not just any army, THE Assyrian army who has conquered every other city in their path and who now possesses all surrounding lands except Jerusalem, Judah. The general rides straight to the heart of town and confronts the king's messengers. The upper pool was a common place, usually near the city center, where water was collected for doing laundry and other household tasks. This was not a private meeting between government officials. This was a public display meant to intimidate.

So, imagine you are living in Jerusalem and you have come out on that particular day to wash clothes and you see the dust fly as the army approaches town.

How might you have been feeling?

You want to talk about fear? They felt it. You want to talk about hopelessness? They were living it. I'm sure many of them were convinced this was the end.

Interestingly, King Hezekiah does not send his army or even a general to square off with Rabshakeh. He sends Eliakim, Shebna and Joah to represent Judah. While these three men served very prominent roles in the king's court, they were not warriors. They were not even military. Eliakim was the person over the household or the palace administrator. I envision a manager or banquet/party planner kind of fellow. Shebna was a scribe; a professional interpreter of the law. We might refer to him as a lawyer in modern terms. Some scholars compare his duties to those of a secretary. And Joah was a recorder, the official historian of Judah. I suppose he was along to take notes! Does this picture seem off balance to anyone else? When I first read this in Isaiah, I thought to myself, "great, these men are going to get their heads chopped off right here in the pages of history and Jerusalem is going down." Not so!

Skip ahead to verse 21. What had Hezekiah instructed these three *not* to do?

Carefully, read what the enemy had to say in Isaiah 36:4-20.

As I read this the first time, the Holy Spirit taught me several principles about the enemy. One, he is real. Two, he knows our weaknesses. And three, he is a liar. The enemy always uses the same major tactic. We see it here, throughout the pages of scripture, and we have experienced it in our own lives as well.

The enemy lies.

As Rabshakeh is speaking, the people are listening. He first tries to convince them they are all alone. He tells them they cannot depend on Egypt or anyone else to fight for them. Lie number one: you are alone.

Then, he misinterprets Hezekiah's reforms and insinuates the people have angered or offended God by tearing down places of worship. Of course, the people only tore down altars to false gods, but the enemy doesn't seem to get that. Rather, he pushes the idea that Hezekiah has probably damaged their favor with the Lord and He is not going to help them now. Lie number two: you've angered God and He doesn't love you anymore.

Lie number three: (personally, the most astonishing) your God sent me. Rabshakeh is just utilizing blatant blasphemy here. In no way had God done any such thing, yet, read verse 10. He actually tries to convince the people this was God's will for them. Scary. There are many among us who desire to do the same. Beware of those who use the name of Christ to justify what He has already declared as wrong.

At this point in the verbal attack the three servants of Hezekiah, who are supposed to be keeping quiet, can no longer hold their tongues.

What did they ask of Rabshakeh in verse 11?

How did Rabshakeh respond in verse 12?

The enemy speaks your language.

Lie number four: turn on the leader. King Hezekiah had proven to be a righteous king and a remnant of God's people had experienced revival and blessing under his leadership. However, the enemy knows if he can't convince us otherwise, he can try to bring us down by manipulating us to turn on one another. Division is powerfully destructive.

And lastly, number five, the lie that promises a better deal. A powerful tool in the enemy's belt is to deceive us into believing the grass is greener on the other side. He tries to convince the people to bring a gift and in exchange the Assyrian king would take them to a land of paradise, a place better than the Promised Land.

Read verses 16-17 and list all the wonderful things the Assyrians promised.

The enemy wants you to believe his lies. He wants to paralyze you in fear and defeat. His desire is always to steal, kill and destroy. He is a master manipulator.

Do you believe a lie that has been planted in your heart and mind by the enemy? If so, get it on paper right here. For the last time, settle the issue. Is it true or is it false?

What emotions do you think Rabshakeh's final questions in verses 18-20 evoked in the people listening?

How did Hezekiah's servants respond? What did they do?

Application:

What questions do you have that cause you to fear?

Sometimes our fear comes because we are asking the wrong question. As we leave today, ask God to strengthen you in the face of fear by asking the only question that matters. **Look up Romans 8:31 and write it here.**

Day Five

Finding the Victory

"And so it was, when King Hezekiah heard it, that he tore his clothes, covered himself in sackcloth, and went into the house of the Lord."
Isaiah 37:1

As I read about Hezekiah's servants returning with gut wrenching news, I am a bit taken back by their reaction. Perhaps I shouldn't be, but I am. They were in serious mourning for their nation. Have you ever experienced such intense conviction, burden or passion? I try to imagine the emotions Hezekiah felt. Yes, he had prepared for this; but the facts were terrifying. The enemy was powerful, strong and ruthless and the good guys were beyond outnumbered. His people faced a very real threat of slavery, starvation or death. This is the same situation his father, Ahaz, had faced years before.

Unfortunately, Ahaz paid tribute to the Assyrians and ignored the prophetic warnings. He failed to believe the promise and turned from the Lord.

If you have been timely in your study, weeks ago I asked you to record the location where the Lord instructed Isaiah to meet with King Ahaz, Hezekiah's biological father. Look back in your study guide at the bottom of page 40 (or Isaiah 7:3) to see it.

I find it ironic that in the same place where Isaiah had warned against disobedience and the coming wrath of Assyria, we've just seen Hezekiah's servants standing toe to toe with that very enemy. On the same ground and in the same manner, the nation of Judah, and especially their king, are faced with impossible circumstances and a choice:

Believe God or don't.

According to the Lord's word after Hezekiah's illness, what would happen to Jerusalem? Look back at the top of page 78 in this study guide for the answer or turn to Isaiah 38:6.

What happens in Isaiah 37:2-4? Also see 2 Chronicles 32:20.

Hezekiah does the only thing he could do — he prays.

How does the Lord answer? (Isaiah 37:5-7)

Read Isaiah 37:8-13. What happened next?

Indeed, Sennacherib heard a rumor and he went home to defend his throne against the Ethiopians.

However, Sennacherib sends word, again, threatening a return to defeat Jerusalem and urging King Hezekiah not to listen to God.

The enemy is relentless, but God is in control.

Again, how does Hezekiah respond to the threats? See verses 14-20. What does his prayer reveal about his character?

Hezekiah was very familiar with the presence of God. God was so real to Him that in verse 14 it says he "spread the letter before the Lord". What a beautiful scene! Imagine the young king on his face in the house of the Lord, the letter spread on the floor. Imagine God above, looking down, eyes locked on the words and ears tuned to Hezekiah's simple and bold cry for deliverance. With great humility, Hezekiah prays for God to hear him, to see him and to save his people. I admire how boldly he acknowledges the severity of the situation before God. He doesn't try to pretend this isn't a big deal. He is open and honest about the reality of the circumstances. He knew only the hand of God could save them. On their own, they were completely and utterly hopeless. He recognizes who God is and asks God to save them, not for their own sake, but for God's glory. Hezekiah's love for God preferred *His* glory above all else.

Hezekiah's example is one to emulate.

Fight the enemy with prayer.

Are you currently battling the enemy? Specifically, list the threats you face.

What emotions have gripped your heart?

In light of today's study so far, how would God have *you* respond?

While Hezekiah was well prepared, he still turned to the Lord in prayer. He did not depend on his own abilities to face the enemy. He knew where to turn and he knew why it was so important. For this king, it was never strictly about Judah's deliverance — it was about the glory of his God. The only thing he knew for sure was that God was on his side.

Sometimes, that is all we can know.

"Then Isaiah the son of Amoz sent to Hezekiah saying, "Thus says the Lord God of Israel..." Isaiah 37:1a

Eventually an answer comes.

Read Isaiah 37:21-35. Use verses 33-35 to summarize what God said concerning the king of Assyria.

The Lord God would not permit even one arrow to fly toward Jerusalem! He would keep his promise. After all the threats and all the lies, the enemy would lose. As the Assyrians army often did to their prisoners of war, God would put a hook in their nose and send them back the way they came. Hezekiah was prepared for a fight, but the battle had been won while he was on his knees.

How did things turn out? (See verses 36-38)

What do you suppose would have happened if Hezekiah had let his fear reign, rather than his faith?

Remember, fear and faith cannot co-exist. One will win out.

How does it encourage you to know that in the face of great opposition and hopeless circumstances, our God is able to overcome and has the power to be victorious?

Just as King Hezekiah had a choice, so do we: believe God or don't.

Finishing the Fight

You may be wondering why God allowed the enemy to get so close. Yes, Jerusalem was saved, but what about the other cities? What about Israel? Why did God not protect them in the same way?

God used the evil Sennacherib to be an instrument of judgment against Israel. They were God's chosen, but they were led into captivity. God used pagan, evil people to bring judgment and chastening to His wayward and rebellious children. He loved them too much to leave them in sin and was too just to ignore it.

The story of Hezekiah exhibits a range of emotions and challenges. Before we read the final part of our text, take a moment to think about how far Judah has come. When we first opened to 2 Chronicles, the nation was unrecognizable as God's chosen people. They were wicked and had become hard towards God. But, God chose to use one young man, a great (often forgotten) king to restore His remnant in Judah. After tremendous revival, God poured out blessing on His people. He performed a spectacular miracle for his servant and faithfully delivered them from their enemy. God established Hezekiah's life and reign as one greater than any other in Judah and honored him as a faithful king. During the reign of King Hezekiah, Judah became living proof that they served the one true God! Make no mistake — the hero of Judah was NOT King Hezekiah. The hero was Almighty God.

Final Application:

How similar most of our stories are to this one. Before we receive Christ, we are unrecognizable as children of the Most High. As we surrender to Him, He changes us, makes us new and sets us up as witnesses of His love and grace for His glory.

Below, list three new things you learned about King Hezekiah through this study:

1)
2)
3)

Most importantly, describe what you have learned about God through this study:

Please look back at the ***question on page 13. Has God provided an answer or clarity for you through His word?

What would God have you do in response to what you have learned?

Finish by reading the final summary of King Hezekiah's life below.

"Thus the Lord saved Hezekiah and the inhabitants of Jerusalem from the hand of Sennacherib the King of Assyria, and from the hand of all others, and guided them on every side. And many brought gifts to the Lord at Jerusalem, and presents to Hezekiah king of Judah, so that he was exalted in the sight of all nations thereafter....

now the rest of the acts of Hezekiah and his goodness, behold, they are written in the vision of Isaiah the prophet, son of Amoz, and in the book of the kings of Judah and Israel.

And Hezekiah slept with his fathers, and they buried him in the chiefest of the sepulchers of the sons of David: and all Judah and the inhabitants of Jerusalem did him honor at his death. And Manasseh his son reigned in his place."

2 Chronicles 32:22-23, 32-33

Praise God for His word! King Hezekiah was an example of a life of bold faith. In the end, *the king was honored and **God was glorified.***

May the same be said of us.

Thank you for joining me on this journey!
Visit me at jaclynrowe.com for more information.

THE KINGDOMS OF ISRAEL AND JUDAH

SCALE OF MILES
0   10   20   30   40

This map can be viewed at:
www.bible.ca
Steven Rudd (2007)

The Great Sea

Sidon
Damascus
KINGDOM OF DAMASCUS
Tyre
Dan
PHOENICIA

ISRAEL
SAMARIA
River Jordan

Joppa
Bethel
AMMON
JERUSALEM
Tokea
Moresheth
Lake Asphaltitis (Dead Sea)

Gaza
PHILISTIA
JUDAH
MOAB

Beersheba

Tharu (Arish)
Wadi el Arish
Egypt

Ain el Quderiat
Kings Highway
Wilderness of Zin
Kadesh Barnea
Petra (Sela)
Mt. Hor

Negev
Judah
Mt. Karkom
Kenites
Wilderness of Paran
Edom

Wilderness of Egypt
Ezek 20:36
Egypt
Elat
Mt. Seir
Ezion Geber
Red Sea

N W E S

SELECTED REFERENCES

I list here only the writings or sources that have been of use in the making of this book. This bibliography is by no means a complete record of all the works and sources I have consulted in the nearly four years of study on this topic. It indicates the substance and range of reading upon which I have formed my ideas. I intend to provide this list as a convenience for those who wish to pursue the study of King Hezekiah and Biblical accounts. Any and all direct quotes are noted within the book.

Alexander, Pat and David. *Zondervan Handbook to the Bible.* England: Lion Publishing, Inc., Michigan: Zondervan, 1999.

Life Application Study Bible: New King James Version. Illinois: Tyndale House Publishing, Inc., 1993.

Rogers, Adrian. *What Every Christian Ought to Know.* Tennessee: B&H Publishing Group, 2012

Vine, W.E.; Unger, Merrill F.; White, William, Jr. *Vine's Complete Expository Dictionary of Old and New Testament Words.* Tennessee: Thomas Nelson, Inc. and distributed in Canada by Nelson/Word of Canada, 1996.

Who's Who in the Bible. New York: The Reader's Digest Association, Inc., 2003.

Wiersbe, Warren W. *The Bible Exposition Commentary: Old Testament History.* Colorado: David C. Cook, 2003.

Scriptures noted ESV, NIV or translations other than NKJV were taken from www.biblegateway.com. 2013.

Aren't you glad you are a Life in Progress?

Learn more about Life in Progress Ministries through jaclynrowe.com.

ABOUT THE AUTHOR

is a wife, mother, ministry leader, national speaker, business owner and author. Her desire is to effectively and passionately use her gifts to expand the kingdom of God. Alongside her husband Nathan, Jaclyn and her brother, Klinton Silvey, recently founded Life in Progress Ministries. The ministry is dedicated to breaking down barriers that keep non-believers out and helping believers learn, love and live the Christian faith.

Raised in a loving Christian home, Jaclyn committed her life to Jesus Christ at a young age. Her faith journey currently finds her in an authentic relationship with the creator of the universe because of her faith in Jesus Christ. She is called and spiritually gifted to teach the living and powerful Word of God. Her enthusiasm for Truth and His love compel her to press on. She has far to go.

Currently, Jaclyn teaches a weekly Bible class for young women, a weekly Bible program for pre-school children and volunteers as a speaker for Stonecroft Ministries. In the fall, Jaclyn will be leading a community-wide women's Bible study featuring *King Hezekiah, Examining a Life of Bold Faith* in her hometown. Jaclyn and her husband also own and operate JNR Pool Construction and Jaclyn speaks on the topics of Personality and American Business Etiquette in the corporate marketplace.

Jaclyn would be honored to speak at your next women's event, conference or retreat.

For more information visit **www.jaclynrowe.com,**
www.lifeinprogressministries.com or write to Jaclyn at
lifeinprogressministries@gmail.com. Of course, you can always find us
on Facebook at www.facebook.com/lipministries.